Dear Doer,
You're holding more than a planner, you're holding a fresh start and a steady guide for the year ahead. This planner is built to help you turn ideas into action, put purposeful rhythm into your marketing, and create real momentum in your business without drowning in the noise.

Inside, you'll find tools to plan smarter, stay consistent, and build a content strategy that fits the actual life you're living. Use it as your anchor each month. Let it hold your goals, your wins, your wild ideas, and the plans that carry you forward. You don't need perfection to succeed, just intention, clarity, and the willingness to keep showing up. This planner helps you do exactly that.

Cheers & happy planning,
Samantha
Founder of the Plandipity Doer's

# THIS PLANNER BELONGS TO

---

## About the Plandipity Doers

The Plandipity Doers was created from two powerful forces: a passion for helping women build sustainable, repeatable systems in their businesses, and the legacy of a woman whose dream was to bring creatives together under one supportive roof.

My mom always wanted to create a collective, a place where artists could thrive year-round, share resources, and grow through community. When she passed on September 10th, over 20 years ago, her dream could have ended there. Instead, it became the spark behind everything I've built. The heart of Plandipity is her belief that entrepreneurs deserve space, support, and a circle that lifts you higher.

Today, the Plandipity Doers is that circle. It's a community shaped for women who are doing the work, balancing business, life, ambition, and the messy middle. Here, we plan with intention, create with confidence, and build momentum through systems that make success feel doable. It's a space where marketing feels lighter, ideas flow more freely, and progress doesn't require perfection, just honest effort and a supportive community behind you.

The mission is simple: empower you to show up with clarity, consistency, and creativity, and to grow in a community where your goals actually feel achievable. My mom wanted a place where artists could flourish. This is my version of bringing that dream to life—one Doer, one plan, one year at a time.

# MY 2026 GOAL PLAN

GOAL

Why it matters:

ACTION STEPS

HABIT

NEW HABITS TO BUILD

WHAT TO LEAVE BEHIND

GOAL

Why it matters:

ACTION STEPS

HABIT

NEW HABITS TO BUILD

WHAT TO LEAVE BEHIND

GOAL

Why it matters:

ACTION STEPS

HABIT

NEW HABITS TO BUILD

WHAT TO LEAVE BEHIND

# 2026

## January

| S | M | T | W | T | F | S |
|---|---|---|---|---|---|---|
| | | | | 1 | 2 | 3 |
| 4 | 5 | 6 | 7 | 8 | 9 | 10 |
| 11 | 12 | 13 | 14 | 15 | 16 | 17 |
| 18 | 19 | 20 | 21 | 22 | 23 | 24 |
| 25 | 26 | 27 | 28 | 29 | 30 | 31 |

## February

| S | M | T | W | T | F | S |
|---|---|---|---|---|---|---|
| 1 | 2 | 3 | 4 | 5 | 6 | 7 |
| 8 | 9 | 10 | 11 | 12 | 13 | 14 |
| 15 | 16 | 17 | 18 | 19 | 20 | 21 |
| 22 | 23 | 24 | 25 | 26 | 27 | 28 |

## March

| S | M | T | W | T | F | S |
|---|---|---|---|---|---|---|
| 1 | 2 | 3 | 4 | 5 | 6 | 7 |
| 8 | 9 | 10 | 11 | 12 | 13 | 14 |
| 15 | 16 | 17 | 18 | 19 | 20 | 21 |
| 22 | 23 | 24 | 25 | 26 | 27 | 28 |
| 29 | 30 | 31 | | | | |

## April

| S | M | T | W | T | F | S |
|---|---|---|---|---|---|---|
| | | | 1 | 2 | 3 | 4 |
| 5 | 6 | 7 | 8 | 9 | 10 | 11 |
| 12 | 13 | 14 | 15 | 16 | 17 | 18 |
| 19 | 20 | 21 | 22 | 23 | 24 | 25 |
| 26 | 27 | 28 | 29 | 30 | | |

## May

| S | M | T | W | T | F | S |
|---|---|---|---|---|---|---|
| | | | | | 1 | 2 |
| 3 | 4 | 5 | 6 | 7 | 8 | 9 |
| 10 | 11 | 12 | 13 | 14 | 15 | 16 |
| 17 | 18 | 19 | 20 | 21 | 22 | 23 |
| 24 | 25 | 26 | 27 | 28 | 29 | 30 |
| 31 | | | | | | |

## June

| S | M | T | W | T | F | S |
|---|---|---|---|---|---|---|
| | 1 | 2 | 3 | 4 | 5 | 6 |
| 7 | 8 | 9 | 10 | 11 | 12 | 13 |
| 14 | 15 | 16 | 17 | 18 | 19 | 20 |
| 21 | 22 | 23 | 24 | 25 | 26 | 27 |
| 28 | 29 | 30 | | | | |

## July

| S | M | T | W | T | F | S |
|---|---|---|---|---|---|---|
| | | | 1 | 2 | 3 | 4 |
| 5 | 6 | 7 | 8 | 9 | 10 | 11 |
| 12 | 13 | 14 | 15 | 16 | 17 | 18 |
| 19 | 20 | 21 | 22 | 23 | 24 | 25 |
| 26 | 27 | 28 | 29 | 30 | 31 | |

## August

| S | M | T | W | T | F | S |
|---|---|---|---|---|---|---|
| | | | | | | 1 |
| 2 | 3 | 4 | 5 | 6 | 7 | 8 |
| 9 | 10 | 11 | 12 | 13 | 14 | 15 |
| 16 | 17 | 18 | 19 | 20 | 21 | 22 |
| 23 | 24 | 25 | 26 | 27 | 28 | 29 |
| 30 | 31 | | | | | |

## September

| S | M | T | W | T | F | S |
|---|---|---|---|---|---|---|
| | | 1 | 2 | 3 | 4 | 5 |
| 6 | 7 | 8 | 9 | 10 | 11 | 12 |
| 13 | 14 | 15 | 16 | 17 | 18 | 29 |
| 20 | 21 | 22 | 23 | 24 | 25 | 26 |
| 27 | 28 | 29 | 30 | | | |

## October

| S | M | T | W | T | F | S |
|---|---|---|---|---|---|---|
| | | | | 1 | 2 | 3 |
| 4 | 5 | 6 | 7 | 8 | 9 | 10 |
| 11 | 12 | 13 | 14 | 15 | 16 | 17 |
| 18 | 19 | 20 | 21 | 22 | 23 | 24 |
| 25 | 26 | 27 | 28 | 29 | 30 | 31 |

## November

| S | M | T | W | T | F | S |
|---|---|---|---|---|---|---|
| 1 | 2 | 3 | 4 | 5 | 6 | 7 |
| 8 | 9 | 10 | 11 | 12 | 13 | 14 |
| 15 | 16 | 17 | 18 | 19 | 20 | 21 |
| 22 | 23 | 24 | 25 | 26 | 27 | 28 |
| 29 | 30 | | | | | |

## December

| S | M | T | W | T | F | S |
|---|---|---|---|---|---|---|
| | | 1 | 2 | 3 | 4 | 5 |
| 6 | 7 | 8 | 9 | 10 | 11 | 12 |
| 13 | 14 | 15 | 16 | 17 | 18 | 19 |
| 20 | 21 | 22 | 23 | 24 | 25 | 26 |
| 27 | 28 | 29 | 30 | 31 | | |

# 2026 Holidays & Fun National Days

## January 2026

| | |
|---|---|
| Jan 1 | New Years Day |
| Jan 14 | National Dress Up Your Pet Day |
| Jan 19 | Martin Luther King Jr. Day |
| Jan 30 | National Fun At Work Day |

## February 2026

| | |
|---|---|
| Feb 1 | National Get Up Day |
| Feb 2 | Groundhog Day |
| Feb 14 | Valentine's Day |
| Feb 16 | Presidents Day |

## March 2026

| | |
|---|---|
| Mar 7 | National Be Heard Day |
| Mar 8 | International Women's Day |
| Mar 8 | Daylight Saving Time Begins |
| Mar 17 | St. Patrick's Day |
| Mar 20 | First Day of Spring |
| Mar 29 | National Mom and Pop Business Owners Day |

## April 2026

| | |
|---|---|
| April 1 | April Fools Day |
| Apr 5 | Easter Sunday |
| Apr 8 | National All Is Ours Day |
| Apr 15 | National Tax Day |
| Apr 22 | Earth Day |
| Apr 23 | National Take a Chance Day |

## May 2026

| | |
|---|---|
| May 1 | May Day |
| May 4 | May The 4TH Be With You - Star Wars Day |
| May 5 | Cinco de Mayo |
| May 10 | Mother's Day |
| May 12 | National Teacher Appreciation Day |
| May 25 | Memorial Day |
| May 30 | National Creativity Day |

## June 2026

| | |
|---|---|
| Jun 2 | National Leave the Office Early Day |
| Jun 19 | Juneteenth National Independence Day |
| Jun 20 | First Day of Summer |
| Jun 21 | Father's Day |
| Jun 21 | National Selfie Day |
| Jun 30 | Social Media Day |

## July 2026

| | |
|---|---|
| Jul 4 | Independence Day |
| Jul 5 | National Workaholics Day |
| Jul 11 | National Simplicity Day |
| Jul 16 | Get to Know Your Customers Day<br>*Third Thursday of each Quarter* |

## August 2026

| | |
|---|---|
| Aug 2 | National Friendship Day |
| Aug 9 | National Book Lovers Day |
| Aug 28 | National Thoughtful Day |

## September 2026

| | |
|---|---|
| Sep 7 | Labor Day |
| Sep 10 | National Plandipity Doer's Day<br>*(applied for)* |
| Sep 11 | Patriot Day |
| Sep 12 | National Day of Encouragement |
| Sep 22 | First Day of Fall |
| Sep 22 | American Business Women's Day |

## October 2026

| | |
|---|---|
| Oct 16 | Boss's Day |
| Oct 21 | Support Your Local Chamber of Commerce Day |
| Oct 24 | National Make A Difference Day |
| Oct 31 | Halloween |

## November 2026

| | |
|---|---|
| Nov 1 | Daylight Saving Time Ends |
| Nov 3 | Election Day |
| Nov 4 | National Stress Awareness Day |
| Nov 11 | Veterans Day |
| Nov 26 | Thanksgiving Day |
| Nov 27 | Native American Heritage Day |
| Nov 28 | Small Business Saturday |

## December 2026

| | |
|---|---|
| Dec 7 | Pearl Harbor Remembrance Day |
| Dec 10 | Hanukkah Begins |
| Dec 18 | Hanukkah Ends |
| Dec 21 | First Day of Winter |
| Dec 25 | Christmas Day |
| Dec 26 | National Thank-You Note Day |

Find more National Days/Weeks/Months to boost your marketing in the monthly Content Caboodle™

"YOU CAN'T TALK YOURSELF INTO A NEW LIFE; *you have to act yourself* INTO ONE."

**JEN SINCERO**

# *January* 2026

# January 2026

## Business Goal

What's the one thing that will move your business forward this month?

## Personal Goal

What personal win or habit will make life easier or happier?

## Social Media Marketing Planning

### KEY DATES

What holidays, launches, or community events should you post about?

### THIS MONTH'S MARKETING FOCUS

### BUSINESS EVENTS

### PERSONAL EVENTS

PLAN WITH ME!

**Need inspiration? Scan the QR code for this month's planning video and let's map it out together!**

## My Tasks This Month

NOTES AND IDEAS

Stop winging it and start planning it. Learn the system that makes content creation feel effortless.

Plan smarter—join the waitlist!

# January 2026

| SUNDAY | MONDAY | TUESDAY | WEDNESDAY |
|---|---|---|---|
| | | | |
| 4 | 5 | 6 | 7 |
| 11 | 12 | 13 | 14 |
| 18 | 19 | 20 | 21 |
| 25 | 26 | 27 | 28 |

| THURSDAY | FRIDAY | SATURDAY |
| --- | --- | --- |
| 1 | 2 | 3 |
| 8 | 9 | 10 |
| 15 | 16 | 17<br>CONTENT CABOODLE DROPS TODAY! |
| 22 | 23 | 24 |
| 29 | 30 | 31 |

## Notes

## Reminders

**Doer's: be sure to register for weekly We Plan Wednesdays**

# January 2026

## TOP TO-DOS THIS WEEK

## FOLLOW UPS

## APPOINTMENTS

MON

TUE

WED

THU

FRI

SAT

SUN

## SOCIAL MEDIA FOCUS/GOAL THIS WEEK

Dear January,
let's make
*'figuring it out'*
look fabulous!

# SOCIAL MEDIA ENGAGEMENT PLAN & TRACKER

ENGAGEMENT ACTIVITY:

| | | SUN | MON | TUE | WED | THU | FRI | SAT |
|---|---|---|---|---|---|---|---|---|
| NOTES: | WK1 | | | | | | | |
| | WK2 | | | | | | | |
| | WK3 | | | | | | | |
| | WK4 | | | | | | | |

ENGAGEMENT ACTIVITY:

| | | SUN | MON | TUE | WED | THU | FRI | SAT |
|---|---|---|---|---|---|---|---|---|
| NOTES: | WK1 | | | | | | | |
| | WK2 | | | | | | | |
| | WK3 | | | | | | | |
| | WK4 | | | | | | | |

ENGAGEMENT ACTIVITY:

| | | SUN | MON | TUE | WED | THU | FRI | SAT |
|---|---|---|---|---|---|---|---|---|
| NOTES: | WK1 | | | | | | | |
| | WK2 | | | | | | | |
| | WK3 | | | | | | | |
| | WK4 | | | | | | | |

ENGAGEMENT ACTIVITY:

| | | SUN | MON | TUE | WED | THU | FRI | SAT |
|---|---|---|---|---|---|---|---|---|
| NOTES: | WK1 | | | | | | | |
| | WK2 | | | | | | | |
| | WK3 | | | | | | | |
| | WK4 | | | | | | | |

ENGAGEMENT ACTIVITY:

| | | SUN | MON | TUE | WED | THU | FRI | SAT |
|---|---|---|---|---|---|---|---|---|
| NOTES: | WK1 | | | | | | | |
| | WK2 | | | | | | | |
| | WK3 | | | | | | | |
| | WK4 | | | | | | | |

# January 2026

MONDAY

TUESDAY

WEDNESDAY

NOTES

1 THURSDAY

New Years Day

2 FRIDAY

3 SATURDAY

4 SUNDAY

# January 2026

## TOP TO-DOS THIS WEEK

- [ ] 
- [ ] 
- [ ] 
- [ ] 
- [ ] 
- [ ] 

## FOLLOW UPS

## APPOINTMENTS

MON

TUE

WED

THU

FRI

SAT

SUN

## SOCIAL MEDIA FOCUS/GOAL THIS WEEK

Small steps still move you forward.

# SOCIAL MEDIA ENGAGEMENT PLAN & TRACKER

ENGAGEMENT ACTIVITY:

| | | SUN | MON | TUE | WED | THU | FRI | SAT |
|---|---|---|---|---|---|---|---|---|
| NOTES: | WK1 | | | | | | | |
| | WK2 | | | | | | | |
| | WK3 | | | | | | | |
| | WK4 | | | | | | | |

ENGAGEMENT ACTIVITY:

| | | SUN | MON | TUE | WED | THU | FRI | SAT |
|---|---|---|---|---|---|---|---|---|
| NOTES: | WK1 | | | | | | | |
| | WK2 | | | | | | | |
| | WK3 | | | | | | | |
| | WK4 | | | | | | | |

ENGAGEMENT ACTIVITY:

| | | SUN | MON | TUE | WED | THU | FRI | SAT |
|---|---|---|---|---|---|---|---|---|
| NOTES: | WK1 | | | | | | | |
| | WK2 | | | | | | | |
| | WK3 | | | | | | | |
| | WK4 | | | | | | | |

ENGAGEMENT ACTIVITY:

| | | SUN | MON | TUE | WED | THU | FRI | SAT |
|---|---|---|---|---|---|---|---|---|
| NOTES: | WK1 | | | | | | | |
| | WK2 | | | | | | | |
| | WK3 | | | | | | | |
| | WK4 | | | | | | | |

ENGAGEMENT ACTIVITY:

| | | SUN | MON | TUE | WED | THU | FRI | SAT |
|---|---|---|---|---|---|---|---|---|
| NOTES: | WK1 | | | | | | | |
| | WK2 | | | | | | | |
| | WK3 | | | | | | | |
| | WK4 | | | | | | | |

# January 2026

5 MONDAY

6 TUESDAY

7 WEDNESDAY

NOTES

8 THURSDAY

9 FRIDAY

10 SATURDAY

11 SUNDAY

# January 2026

## TOP TO-DOS THIS WEEK

- [ ] 
- [ ] 
- [ ] 
- [ ] 
- [ ] 
- [ ] 

## FOLLOW UPS

## APPOINTMENTS

MON

TUE

WED

THU

FRI

SAT

SUN

## SOCIAL MEDIA FOCUS/GOAL THIS WEEK

New year,
same me -
just better boundaries
and stronger coffee.

# SOCIAL MEDIA ENGAGEMENT PLAN & TRACKER

ENGAGEMENT ACTIVITY:

| | | SUN | MON | TUE | WED | THU | FRI | SAT |
|---|---|---|---|---|---|---|---|---|
| NOTES: | WK1 | | | | | | | |
| | WK2 | | | | | | | |
| | WK3 | | | | | | | |
| | WK4 | | | | | | | |

ENGAGEMENT ACTIVITY:

| | | SUN | MON | TUE | WED | THU | FRI | SAT |
|---|---|---|---|---|---|---|---|---|
| NOTES: | WK1 | | | | | | | |
| | WK2 | | | | | | | |
| | WK3 | | | | | | | |
| | WK4 | | | | | | | |

ENGAGEMENT ACTIVITY:

| | | SUN | MON | TUE | WED | THU | FRI | SAT |
|---|---|---|---|---|---|---|---|---|
| NOTES: | WK1 | | | | | | | |
| | WK2 | | | | | | | |
| | WK3 | | | | | | | |
| | WK4 | | | | | | | |

ENGAGEMENT ACTIVITY:

| | | SUN | MON | TUE | WED | THU | FRI | SAT |
|---|---|---|---|---|---|---|---|---|
| NOTES: | WK1 | | | | | | | |
| | WK2 | | | | | | | |
| | WK3 | | | | | | | |
| | WK4 | | | | | | | |

ENGAGEMENT ACTIVITY:

| | | SUN | MON | TUE | WED | THU | FRI | SAT |
|---|---|---|---|---|---|---|---|---|
| NOTES: | WK1 | | | | | | | |
| | WK2 | | | | | | | |
| | WK3 | | | | | | | |
| | WK4 | | | | | | | |

# January 2026

12 MONDAY

13 TUESDAY

14 WEDNESDAY

National Dress Up Your Pet Day

NOTES

15 THURSDAY

16 FRIDAY

17 SATURDAY

18 SUNDAY

# January 2026

## TOP TO-DOS THIS WEEK

## FOLLOW UPS

## APPOINTMENTS

MON

TUE

WED

THU

FRI

SAT

SUN

## SOCIAL MEDIA FOCUS/GOAL THIS WEEK

Ignore the voice that doubts you– it's **never** built a damn thing!

# SOCIAL MEDIA ENGAGEMENT PLAN & TRACKER

ENGAGEMENT ACTIVITY:

| | | SUN | MON | TUE | WED | THU | FRI | SAT |
|---|---|---|---|---|---|---|---|---|
| NOTES: | WK1 | | | | | | | |
| | WK2 | | | | | | | |
| | WK3 | | | | | | | |
| | WK4 | | | | | | | |

ENGAGEMENT ACTIVITY:

| | | SUN | MON | TUE | WED | THU | FRI | SAT |
|---|---|---|---|---|---|---|---|---|
| NOTES: | WK1 | | | | | | | |
| | WK2 | | | | | | | |
| | WK3 | | | | | | | |
| | WK4 | | | | | | | |

ENGAGEMENT ACTIVITY:

| | | SUN | MON | TUE | WED | THU | FRI | SAT |
|---|---|---|---|---|---|---|---|---|
| NOTES: | WK1 | | | | | | | |
| | WK2 | | | | | | | |
| | WK3 | | | | | | | |
| | WK4 | | | | | | | |

ENGAGEMENT ACTIVITY:

| | | SUN | MON | TUE | WED | THU | FRI | SAT |
|---|---|---|---|---|---|---|---|---|
| NOTES: | WK1 | | | | | | | |
| | WK2 | | | | | | | |
| | WK3 | | | | | | | |
| | WK4 | | | | | | | |

ENGAGEMENT ACTIVITY:

| | | SUN | MON | TUE | WED | THU | FRI | SAT |
|---|---|---|---|---|---|---|---|---|
| NOTES: | WK1 | | | | | | | |
| | WK2 | | | | | | | |
| | WK3 | | | | | | | |
| | WK4 | | | | | | | |

# January 2026

19 MONDAY

Martin Luther King Jr. Day

20 TUESDAY

21 WEDNESDAY

NOTES

22 THURSDAY

23 FRIDAY

24 SATURDAY

25 SUNDAY

# January 2026

## TOP TO-DOS THIS WEEK

## FOLLOW UPS

## APPOINTMENTS

MON

TUE

WED

THU

FRI

SAT

SUN

## SOCIAL MEDIA FOCUS/GOAL THIS WEEK

Manifesting is cute,
but have
you tried doing
the damn work?

# SOCIAL MEDIA ENGAGEMENT PLAN & TRACKER

ENGAGEMENT ACTIVITY:

| | | SUN | MON | TUE | WED | THU | FRI | SAT |
|---|---|---|---|---|---|---|---|---|
| NOTES: | WK1 | | | | | | | |
| | WK2 | | | | | | | |
| | WK3 | | | | | | | |
| | WK4 | | | | | | | |

ENGAGEMENT ACTIVITY:

| | | SUN | MON | TUE | WED | THU | FRI | SAT |
|---|---|---|---|---|---|---|---|---|
| NOTES: | WK1 | | | | | | | |
| | WK2 | | | | | | | |
| | WK3 | | | | | | | |
| | WK4 | | | | | | | |

ENGAGEMENT ACTIVITY:

| | | SUN | MON | TUE | WED | THU | FRI | SAT |
|---|---|---|---|---|---|---|---|---|
| NOTES: | WK1 | | | | | | | |
| | WK2 | | | | | | | |
| | WK3 | | | | | | | |
| | WK4 | | | | | | | |

ENGAGEMENT ACTIVITY:

| | | SUN | MON | TUE | WED | THU | FRI | SAT |
|---|---|---|---|---|---|---|---|---|
| NOTES: | WK1 | | | | | | | |
| | WK2 | | | | | | | |
| | WK3 | | | | | | | |
| | WK4 | | | | | | | |

ENGAGEMENT ACTIVITY:

| | | SUN | MON | TUE | WED | THU | FRI | SAT |
|---|---|---|---|---|---|---|---|---|
| NOTES: | WK1 | | | | | | | |
| | WK2 | | | | | | | |
| | WK3 | | | | | | | |
| | WK4 | | | | | | | |

# January 2026

26 MONDAY

27 TUESDAY

28 WEDNESDAY

NOTES

29 THURSDAY

30 FRIDAY

National Fun At Work Day

31 SATURDAY

1 SUNDAY

National Get Up Day

# January 2026

## MONTH IN REVIEW

I AM GRATEFUL FOR

CONNECTED WITH

PERSONAL WINS

WHAT I LEARNED

GOALS MET

PREFERED PLATFORM GROWTH

TOP PERFORMING POST

Doer's- Share your a-ha's for the month in the Plandipity Doer's Inner Circle (Our Private FB Group)

"I ALWAYS DID SOMETHING I WAS A LITTLE NOT READY TO DO.

*I think that's how you grow."*

**MARISSA MAYER**

# *February* 2026

# February 2026

## Business Goal

What's the one thing that will move your business forward this month?

## Personal Goal

What personal win or habit will make life easier or happier?

## Social Media Marketing Planning

### KEY DATES

What holidays, launches, or community events should you post about?

- ______________________________
- ______________________________
- ______________________________
- ______________________________
- ______________________________

### THIS MONTH'S MARKETING FOCUS

### BUSINESS EVENTS

### PERSONAL EVENTS

**Let's plan your content with heart and strategy !**
**Scan the QR code and join me for this month's planning video!**

## My Tasks This Month

NOTES AND IDEAS

You don't have to do it alone. Join the community where consistency actually feels fun.

Join the Doers and grow together.

# February 2026

| SUNDAY | MONDAY | TUESDAY | WEDNESDAY |
|---|---|---|---|
| 1 | 2 | 3 | 4 |
| 8 | 9 | 10 | 11 |
| 15 | 16 | 17 | 18 |
| 22 | 23 | 24 | 25 |
| 1 | 2 | 3 | 4 |

| THURSDAY | FRIDAY | SATURDAY |
| --- | --- | --- |
| 5 | 6 | 7 |
| 12 | 13 | 14 |
| 19 | 20 | 21<br>CONTENT CABOODLE DROPS TODAY! |
| 26 | 27 | 28 |
| 5 | 6 | 7 |

Notes

Reminders

Doer's: be sure to register for weekly We Plan Wednesdays

# February 2026

## TOP TO-DOS THIS WEEK

- [ ]
- [ ]
- [ ]
- [ ]
- [ ]
- [ ]

## FOLLOW UPS

## APPOINTMENTS

MON

TUE

WED

THU

FRI

SAT

SUN

## SOCIAL MEDIA FOCUS/GOAL THIS WEEK

Do it scared,
**Do It**
anyway!

# SOCIAL MEDIA ENGAGEMENT PLAN & TRACKER

ENGAGEMENT ACTIVITY:

| | | SUN | MON | TUE | WED | THU | FRI | SAT |
|---|---|---|---|---|---|---|---|---|
| NOTES: | WK1 | | | | | | | |
| | WK2 | | | | | | | |
| | WK3 | | | | | | | |
| | WK4 | | | | | | | |

ENGAGEMENT ACTIVITY:

| | | SUN | MON | TUE | WED | THU | FRI | SAT |
|---|---|---|---|---|---|---|---|---|
| NOTES: | WK1 | | | | | | | |
| | WK2 | | | | | | | |
| | WK3 | | | | | | | |
| | WK4 | | | | | | | |

ENGAGEMENT ACTIVITY:

| | | SUN | MON | TUE | WED | THU | FRI | SAT |
|---|---|---|---|---|---|---|---|---|
| NOTES: | WK1 | | | | | | | |
| | WK2 | | | | | | | |
| | WK3 | | | | | | | |
| | WK4 | | | | | | | |

ENGAGEMENT ACTIVITY:

| | | SUN | MON | TUE | WED | THU | FRI | SAT |
|---|---|---|---|---|---|---|---|---|
| NOTES: | WK1 | | | | | | | |
| | WK2 | | | | | | | |
| | WK3 | | | | | | | |
| | WK4 | | | | | | | |

ENGAGEMENT ACTIVITY:

| | | SUN | MON | TUE | WED | THU | FRI | SAT |
|---|---|---|---|---|---|---|---|---|
| NOTES: | WK1 | | | | | | | |
| | WK2 | | | | | | | |
| | WK3 | | | | | | | |
| | WK4 | | | | | | | |

# February 2026

2 MONDAY

Groundhog Day

3 TUESDAY

4 WEDNESDAY

NOTES

5 THURSDAY

6 FRIDAY

7 SATURDAY

8 SUNDAY

# February 2026

## TOP TO-DOS THIS WEEK

## FOLLOW UPS

## APPOINTMENTS

MON

TUE

WED

THU

FRI

SAT

SUN

## SOCIAL MEDIA FOCUS/GOAL THIS WEEK

Commitment is love for your future self, shown through what you do today.

# SOCIAL MEDIA ENGAGEMENT PLAN & TRACKER

ENGAGEMENT ACTIVITY:

| | | SUN | MON | TUE | WED | THU | FRI | SAT |
|---|---|---|---|---|---|---|---|---|
| NOTES: | WK1 | | | | | | | |
| | WK2 | | | | | | | |
| | WK3 | | | | | | | |
| | WK4 | | | | | | | |

ENGAGEMENT ACTIVITY:

| | | SUN | MON | TUE | WED | THU | FRI | SAT |
|---|---|---|---|---|---|---|---|---|
| NOTES: | WK1 | | | | | | | |
| | WK2 | | | | | | | |
| | WK3 | | | | | | | |
| | WK4 | | | | | | | |

ENGAGEMENT ACTIVITY:

| | | SUN | MON | TUE | WED | THU | FRI | SAT |
|---|---|---|---|---|---|---|---|---|
| NOTES: | WK1 | | | | | | | |
| | WK2 | | | | | | | |
| | WK3 | | | | | | | |
| | WK4 | | | | | | | |

ENGAGEMENT ACTIVITY:

| | | SUN | MON | TUE | WED | THU | FRI | SAT |
|---|---|---|---|---|---|---|---|---|
| NOTES: | WK1 | | | | | | | |
| | WK2 | | | | | | | |
| | WK3 | | | | | | | |
| | WK4 | | | | | | | |

ENGAGEMENT ACTIVITY:

| | | SUN | MON | TUE | WED | THU | FRI | SAT |
|---|---|---|---|---|---|---|---|---|
| NOTES: | WK1 | | | | | | | |
| | WK2 | | | | | | | |
| | WK3 | | | | | | | |
| | WK4 | | | | | | | |

# February 2026

9 MONDAY

10 TUESDAY

11 WEDNESDAY

NOTES

12 THURSDAY

13 FRIDAY

14 SATURDAY

XOXO Valentine's Day

15 SUNDAY

# February 2026

## TOP TO-DOS THIS WEEK

- [ ] 
- [ ] 
- [ ] 
- [ ] 
- [ ] 
- [ ] 

## FOLLOW UPS

## APPOINTMENTS

MON

TUE

WED

THU

FRI

SAT

SUN

## SOCIAL MEDIA FOCUS/GOAL THIS WEEK

You've got everything you need to get started.

# SOCIAL MEDIA ENGAGEMENT PLAN & TRACKER

ENGAGEMENT ACTIVITY:

| | | SUN | MON | TUE | WED | THU | FRI | SAT |
|---|---|---|---|---|---|---|---|---|
| NOTES: | WK1 | | | | | | | |
| | WK2 | | | | | | | |
| | WK3 | | | | | | | |
| | WK4 | | | | | | | |

ENGAGEMENT ACTIVITY:

| | | SUN | MON | TUE | WED | THU | FRI | SAT |
|---|---|---|---|---|---|---|---|---|
| NOTES: | WK1 | | | | | | | |
| | WK2 | | | | | | | |
| | WK3 | | | | | | | |
| | WK4 | | | | | | | |

ENGAGEMENT ACTIVITY:

| | | SUN | MON | TUE | WED | THU | FRI | SAT |
|---|---|---|---|---|---|---|---|---|
| NOTES: | WK1 | | | | | | | |
| | WK2 | | | | | | | |
| | WK3 | | | | | | | |
| | WK4 | | | | | | | |

ENGAGEMENT ACTIVITY:

| | | SUN | MON | TUE | WED | THU | FRI | SAT |
|---|---|---|---|---|---|---|---|---|
| NOTES: | WK1 | | | | | | | |
| | WK2 | | | | | | | |
| | WK3 | | | | | | | |
| | WK4 | | | | | | | |

ENGAGEMENT ACTIVITY:

| | | SUN | MON | TUE | WED | THU | FRI | SAT |
|---|---|---|---|---|---|---|---|---|
| NOTES: | WK1 | | | | | | | |
| | WK2 | | | | | | | |
| | WK3 | | | | | | | |
| | WK4 | | | | | | | |

# February 2026

16 MONDAY

Presidents Day

17 TUESDAY

18 WEDNESDAY

NOTES

19 THURSDAY

20 FRIDAY

21 SATURDAY

22 SUNDAY

# February 2026

## TOP TO-DOS THIS WEEK

## FOLLOW UPS

## APPOINTMENTS

MON

TUE

WED

THU

FRI

SAT

SUN

## SOCIAL MEDIA FOCUS/GOAL THIS WEEK

Keep showing up,
especially
when it's messy.
That's where growth hides.

# SOCIAL MEDIA ENGAGEMENT PLAN & TRACKER

ENGAGEMENT ACTIVITY:

| | | SUN | MON | TUE | WED | THU | FRI | SAT |
|---|---|---|---|---|---|---|---|---|
| NOTES: | WK1 | | | | | | | |
| | WK2 | | | | | | | |
| | WK3 | | | | | | | |
| | WK4 | | | | | | | |

ENGAGEMENT ACTIVITY:

| | | SUN | MON | TUE | WED | THU | FRI | SAT |
|---|---|---|---|---|---|---|---|---|
| NOTES: | WK1 | | | | | | | |
| | WK2 | | | | | | | |
| | WK3 | | | | | | | |
| | WK4 | | | | | | | |

ENGAGEMENT ACTIVITY:

| | | SUN | MON | TUE | WED | THU | FRI | SAT |
|---|---|---|---|---|---|---|---|---|
| NOTES: | WK1 | | | | | | | |
| | WK2 | | | | | | | |
| | WK3 | | | | | | | |
| | WK4 | | | | | | | |

ENGAGEMENT ACTIVITY:

| | | SUN | MON | TUE | WED | THU | FRI | SAT |
|---|---|---|---|---|---|---|---|---|
| NOTES: | WK1 | | | | | | | |
| | WK2 | | | | | | | |
| | WK3 | | | | | | | |
| | WK4 | | | | | | | |

ENGAGEMENT ACTIVITY:

| | | SUN | MON | TUE | WED | THU | FRI | SAT |
|---|---|---|---|---|---|---|---|---|
| NOTES: | WK1 | | | | | | | |
| | WK2 | | | | | | | |
| | WK3 | | | | | | | |
| | WK4 | | | | | | | |

# February 2026

23 MONDAY

24 TUESDAY

25 WEDNESDAY

NOTES

26 THURSDAY

27 FRIDAY

28 SATURDAY

1 SUNDAY

# February 2026

## MONTH IN REVIEW

### I AM GRATEFUL FOR

### CONNECTED WITH

### PERSONAL WINS

### WHAT I LEARNED

### GOALS MET

### PREFERED PLATFORM GROWTH

### TOP PERFORMING POST

Doers — share the love: post your best "lightbulb moment" from this month in the Plandipity Doer's Inner Circle (Our Private FB Group)

"MY BEST SUCCESSES CAME ON
THE HEELS OF FAILURE.
EVERY NO LED ME *closer to a yes.*"

BARBARA CORCORAN

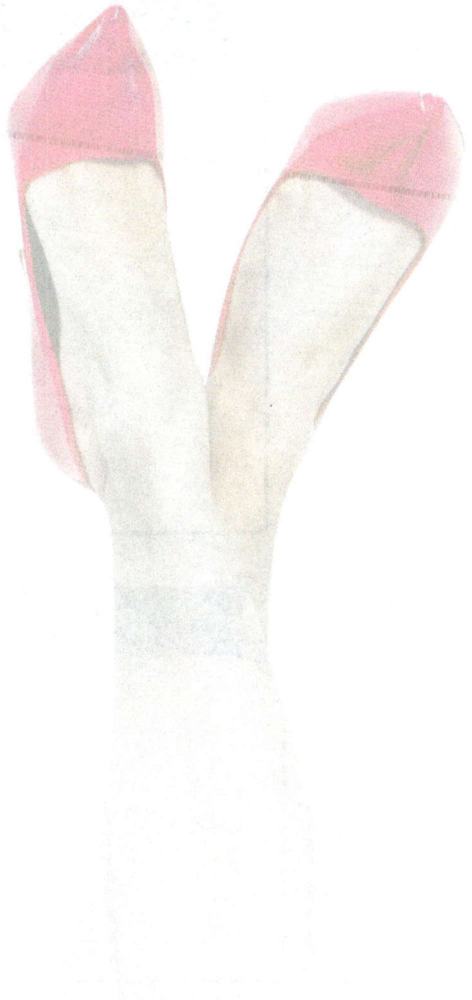

# *March* 2026

# March 2026

## Business Goal

What's the one thing that will move your business forward this month?

## Personal Goal

What personal win or habit will make life easier or happier?

## Social Media Marketing Planning

### KEY DATES

What holidays, launches, or community events should you post about?

### THIS MONTH'S MARKETING FOCUS

### BUSINESS EVENTS

### PERSONAL EVENTS

PLAN WITH ME!

**Ready to kick your content up a notch?**
**Scan the QR code and plan this month's social media with me!**

# My Tasks This Month

## NOTES AND IDEAS

# March 2026

| SUNDAY | MONDAY | TUESDAY | WEDNESDAY |
|---|---|---|---|
| 1 | 2 | 3 | 4 |
| 8 | 9 | 10 | 11 |
| 15 | 16 | 17 | 18 |
| 22 | 23 | 24 | 25 |
| 29 | 30 | 31 | 1 |

| THURSDAY | FRIDAY | SATURDAY |
|---|---|---|
| 5 | 6 | 7 |
| 12 | 13 | 14 |
| 19 | 20 | 21<br>CONTENT CABOODLE DROPS TODAY! |
| 26 | 27 | 28 |
| 2 | 3 | 4 |

## Notes

## Reminders

**Doer's: be sure to register for weekly We Plan Wednesdays**

# March 2026

## TOP TO-DOS THIS WEEK

## FOLLOW UPS

## APPOINTMENTS

MON

TUE

WED

THU

FRI

SAT

SUN

## SOCIAL MEDIA FOCUS/GOAL THIS WEEK

Turn every no into next.

# SOCIAL MEDIA ENGAGEMENT PLAN & TRACKER

ENGAGEMENT ACTIVITY:

| | | SUN | MON | TUE | WED | THU | FRI | SAT |
|---|---|---|---|---|---|---|---|---|
| NOTES: | WK1 | | | | | | | |
| | WK2 | | | | | | | |
| | WK3 | | | | | | | |
| | WK4 | | | | | | | |

ENGAGEMENT ACTIVITY:

| | | SUN | MON | TUE | WED | THU | FRI | SAT |
|---|---|---|---|---|---|---|---|---|
| NOTES: | WK1 | | | | | | | |
| | WK2 | | | | | | | |
| | WK3 | | | | | | | |
| | WK4 | | | | | | | |

ENGAGEMENT ACTIVITY:

| | | SUN | MON | TUE | WED | THU | FRI | SAT |
|---|---|---|---|---|---|---|---|---|
| NOTES: | WK1 | | | | | | | |
| | WK2 | | | | | | | |
| | WK3 | | | | | | | |
| | WK4 | | | | | | | |

ENGAGEMENT ACTIVITY:

| | | SUN | MON | TUE | WED | THU | FRI | SAT |
|---|---|---|---|---|---|---|---|---|
| NOTES: | WK1 | | | | | | | |
| | WK2 | | | | | | | |
| | WK3 | | | | | | | |
| | WK4 | | | | | | | |

ENGAGEMENT ACTIVITY:

| | | SUN | MON | TUE | WED | THU | FRI | SAT |
|---|---|---|---|---|---|---|---|---|
| NOTES: | WK1 | | | | | | | |
| | WK2 | | | | | | | |
| | WK3 | | | | | | | |
| | WK4 | | | | | | | |

# March 2026

2 MONDAY

3 TUESDAY

4 WEDNESDAY

NOTES

5 THURSDAY

6 FRIDAY

7 SATURDAY

National Be Heard Day

8 SUNDAY

International Women's Day

Daylight Saving Time Begins

# March 2026

## TOP TO-DOS THIS WEEK

## FOLLOW UPS

## APPOINTMENTS

MON

TUE

WED

THU

FRI

SAT

SUN

## SOCIAL MEDIA FOCUS/GOAL THIS WEEK

Begin before you're ready;
courage always shows up late but never uninvited.

## SOCIAL MEDIA ENGAGEMENT PLAN & TRACKER

ENGAGEMENT ACTIVITY:

| | | SUN | MON | TUE | WED | THU | FRI | SAT |
|---|---|---|---|---|---|---|---|---|
| NOTES: | WK1 | | | | | | | |
| | WK2 | | | | | | | |
| | WK3 | | | | | | | |
| | WK4 | | | | | | | |

ENGAGEMENT ACTIVITY:

| | | SUN | MON | TUE | WED | THU | FRI | SAT |
|---|---|---|---|---|---|---|---|---|
| NOTES: | WK1 | | | | | | | |
| | WK2 | | | | | | | |
| | WK3 | | | | | | | |
| | WK4 | | | | | | | |

ENGAGEMENT ACTIVITY:

| | | SUN | MON | TUE | WED | THU | FRI | SAT |
|---|---|---|---|---|---|---|---|---|
| NOTES: | WK1 | | | | | | | |
| | WK2 | | | | | | | |
| | WK3 | | | | | | | |
| | WK4 | | | | | | | |

ENGAGEMENT ACTIVITY:

| | | SUN | MON | TUE | WED | THU | FRI | SAT |
|---|---|---|---|---|---|---|---|---|
| NOTES: | WK1 | | | | | | | |
| | WK2 | | | | | | | |
| | WK3 | | | | | | | |
| | WK4 | | | | | | | |

ENGAGEMENT ACTIVITY:

| | | SUN | MON | TUE | WED | THU | FRI | SAT |
|---|---|---|---|---|---|---|---|---|
| NOTES: | WK1 | | | | | | | |
| | WK2 | | | | | | | |
| | WK3 | | | | | | | |
| | WK4 | | | | | | | |

# March 2026

9 MONDAY

10 TUESDAY

11 WEDNESDAY

NOTES

12 THURSDAY

13 FRIDAY

14 SATURDAY

15 SUNDAY

# March 2026

## TOP TO-DOS THIS WEEK

## FOLLOW UPS

## APPOINTMENTS

MON

TUE

WED

THU

FRI

SAT

SUN

## SOCIAL MEDIA FOCUS/GOAL THIS WEEK

Fall down,
rise fierce,
keep shining.

# SOCIAL MEDIA ENGAGEMENT PLAN & TRACKER

ENGAGEMENT ACTIVITY:

| | | SUN | MON | TUE | WED | THU | FRI | SAT |
|---|---|---|---|---|---|---|---|---|
| NOTES: | WK1 | | | | | | | |
| | WK2 | | | | | | | |
| | WK3 | | | | | | | |
| | WK4 | | | | | | | |

ENGAGEMENT ACTIVITY:

| | | SUN | MON | TUE | WED | THU | FRI | SAT |
|---|---|---|---|---|---|---|---|---|
| NOTES: | WK1 | | | | | | | |
| | WK2 | | | | | | | |
| | WK3 | | | | | | | |
| | WK4 | | | | | | | |

ENGAGEMENT ACTIVITY:

| | | SUN | MON | TUE | WED | THU | FRI | SAT |
|---|---|---|---|---|---|---|---|---|
| NOTES: | WK1 | | | | | | | |
| | WK2 | | | | | | | |
| | WK3 | | | | | | | |
| | WK4 | | | | | | | |

ENGAGEMENT ACTIVITY:

| | | SUN | MON | TUE | WED | THU | FRI | SAT |
|---|---|---|---|---|---|---|---|---|
| NOTES: | WK1 | | | | | | | |
| | WK2 | | | | | | | |
| | WK3 | | | | | | | |
| | WK4 | | | | | | | |

ENGAGEMENT ACTIVITY:

| | | SUN | MON | TUE | WED | THU | FRI | SAT |
|---|---|---|---|---|---|---|---|---|
| NOTES: | WK1 | | | | | | | |
| | WK2 | | | | | | | |
| | WK3 | | | | | | | |
| | WK4 | | | | | | | |

# March 2026

16 MONDAY

17 TUESDAY

St. Patrick's Day

18 WEDNESDAY

NOTES

19 THURSDAY

20 FRIDAY

First Day of Spring

21 SATURDAY

22 SUNDAY

# March 2026

## TOP TO-DOS THIS WEEK

- [ ] 
- [ ] 
- [ ] 
- [ ] 
- [ ] 
- [ ] 

## FOLLOW UPS

## APPOINTMENTS

MON

TUE

WED

THU

FRI

SAT

SUN

## SOCIAL MEDIA FOCUS/GOAL THIS WEEK

You're *stronger* than your setbacks.

## SOCIAL MEDIA ENGAGEMENT PLAN & TRACKER

ENGAGEMENT ACTIVITY:

| | | SUN | MON | TUE | WED | THU | FRI | SAT |
|---|---|---|---|---|---|---|---|---|
| NOTES: | WK1 | | | | | | | |
| | WK2 | | | | | | | |
| | WK3 | | | | | | | |
| | WK4 | | | | | | | |

ENGAGEMENT ACTIVITY:

| | | SUN | MON | TUE | WED | THU | FRI | SAT |
|---|---|---|---|---|---|---|---|---|
| NOTES: | WK1 | | | | | | | |
| | WK2 | | | | | | | |
| | WK3 | | | | | | | |
| | WK4 | | | | | | | |

ENGAGEMENT ACTIVITY:

| | | SUN | MON | TUE | WED | THU | FRI | SAT |
|---|---|---|---|---|---|---|---|---|
| NOTES: | WK1 | | | | | | | |
| | WK2 | | | | | | | |
| | WK3 | | | | | | | |
| | WK4 | | | | | | | |

ENGAGEMENT ACTIVITY:

| | | SUN | MON | TUE | WED | THU | FRI | SAT |
|---|---|---|---|---|---|---|---|---|
| NOTES: | WK1 | | | | | | | |
| | WK2 | | | | | | | |
| | WK3 | | | | | | | |
| | WK4 | | | | | | | |

ENGAGEMENT ACTIVITY:

| | | SUN | MON | TUE | WED | THU | FRI | SAT |
|---|---|---|---|---|---|---|---|---|
| NOTES: | WK1 | | | | | | | |
| | WK2 | | | | | | | |
| | WK3 | | | | | | | |
| | WK4 | | | | | | | |

# March 2026

23 MONDAY

24 TUESDAY

25 WEDNESDAY

NOTES

26 THURSDAY

27 FRIDAY

28 SATURDAY

29 SUNDAY

National Mom and Pop Business Owners Day

# March 2026

## TOP TO-DOS THIS WEEK

## FOLLOW UPS

## APPOINTMENTS

MON

TUE

WED

THU

FRI

SAT

SUN

## SOCIAL MEDIA FOCUS/GOAL THIS WEEK

Keep showing up until showing up works.

## SOCIAL MEDIA ENGAGEMENT PLAN & TRACKER

ENGAGEMENT ACTIVITY:

| | | SUN | MON | TUE | WED | THU | FRI | SAT |
|---|---|---|---|---|---|---|---|---|
| NOTES: | WK1 | | | | | | | |
| | WK2 | | | | | | | |
| | WK3 | | | | | | | |
| | WK4 | | | | | | | |

ENGAGEMENT ACTIVITY:

| | | SUN | MON | TUE | WED | THU | FRI | SAT |
|---|---|---|---|---|---|---|---|---|
| NOTES: | WK1 | | | | | | | |
| | WK2 | | | | | | | |
| | WK3 | | | | | | | |
| | WK4 | | | | | | | |

ENGAGEMENT ACTIVITY:

| | | SUN | MON | TUE | WED | THU | FRI | SAT |
|---|---|---|---|---|---|---|---|---|
| NOTES: | WK1 | | | | | | | |
| | WK2 | | | | | | | |
| | WK3 | | | | | | | |
| | WK4 | | | | | | | |

ENGAGEMENT ACTIVITY:

| | | SUN | MON | TUE | WED | THU | FRI | SAT |
|---|---|---|---|---|---|---|---|---|
| NOTES: | WK1 | | | | | | | |
| | WK2 | | | | | | | |
| | WK3 | | | | | | | |
| | WK4 | | | | | | | |

ENGAGEMENT ACTIVITY:

| | | SUN | MON | TUE | WED | THU | FRI | SAT |
|---|---|---|---|---|---|---|---|---|
| NOTES: | WK1 | | | | | | | |
| | WK2 | | | | | | | |
| | WK3 | | | | | | | |
| | WK4 | | | | | | | |

# March 2026

30 MONDAY

31 TUESDAY

1 WEDNESDAY

April Fools Day

NOTES

2 THURSDAY

3 FRIDAY

4 SATURDAY

5 SUNDAY

Happy Easter

# March 2026

## MONTH IN REVIEW

### I AM GRATEFUL FOR

### CONNECTED WITH

### PERSONAL WINS

### WHAT I LEARNED

### GOALS MET

### PREFERED PLATFORM GROWTH

### TOP PERFORMING POST

Doers — momentum check! Tell us your March breakthrough in the Plandipity Doer's Inner Circle (Our Private FB Group)

@MORETHANSERENDIPITY

"SUCCESS IS OFTEN ACHIEVED BY THOSE WHO DON'T KNOW THAT *failure is inevitable.* NAIVETY IS UNDERRATED."

COCO CHANEL

# *April* 2026

# April 2026

## Business Goal

What's the one thing that will move your business forward this month?

## Personal Goal

What personal win or habit will make life easier or happier?

## Social Media Marketing Planning

### KEY DATES

What holidays, launches, or community events should you post about?

- [ ] 
- [ ] 
- [ ] 
- [ ] 
- [ ] 

### THIS MONTH'S MARKETING FOCUS

### BUSINESS EVENTS

### PERSONAL EVENTS

**New quarter, new goals — let's get intentional!**
**Scan the QR code for this month's planning session.**

# My Tasks This Month

NOTES AND IDEAS

Spring is the season for shaking off the chaos—join the Plandipity Doers and get the tools, community, and momentum that make content feel a whole lot lighter.

# April 2026

| SUNDAY | MONDAY | TUESDAY | WEDNESDAY |
| --- | --- | --- | --- |
| 29 | 30 | 31 | 1 |
| 5 | 6 | 7 | 8 |
| 12 | 13 | 14 | 15 |
| 19 | 20 | 21 | 22 |
| 26 | 27 | 28 | 29 |

| THURSDAY | FRIDAY | SATURDAY |
| --- | --- | --- |
| 2 | 3 | 4 |
| 9 | 10 | 11 |
| 16 | 17 | 18<br>CONTENT CABOODLE DROPS TODAY! |
| 23 | 24 | 25 |
| 30 | 1 | 2 |

## Notes

## Reminders

Doer's: be sure to register for weekly We Plan Wednesdays

# April 2026

## TOP TO-DOS THIS WEEK

## FOLLOW UPS

## APPOINTMENTS

MON

TUE

WED

THU

FRI

SAT

SUN

## SOCIAL MEDIA FOCUS/GOAL THIS WEEK

Be bold enough to begin again!

## SOCIAL MEDIA ENGAGEMENT PLAN & TRACKER

ENGAGEMENT ACTIVITY:

| | | SUN | MON | TUE | WED | THU | FRI | SAT |
|---|---|---|---|---|---|---|---|---|
| NOTES: | WK1 | | | | | | | |
| | WK2 | | | | | | | |
| | WK3 | | | | | | | |
| | WK4 | | | | | | | |

ENGAGEMENT ACTIVITY:

| | | SUN | MON | TUE | WED | THU | FRI | SAT |
|---|---|---|---|---|---|---|---|---|
| NOTES: | WK1 | | | | | | | |
| | WK2 | | | | | | | |
| | WK3 | | | | | | | |
| | WK4 | | | | | | | |

ENGAGEMENT ACTIVITY:

| | | SUN | MON | TUE | WED | THU | FRI | SAT |
|---|---|---|---|---|---|---|---|---|
| NOTES: | WK1 | | | | | | | |
| | WK2 | | | | | | | |
| | WK3 | | | | | | | |
| | WK4 | | | | | | | |

ENGAGEMENT ACTIVITY:

| | | SUN | MON | TUE | WED | THU | FRI | SAT |
|---|---|---|---|---|---|---|---|---|
| NOTES: | WK1 | | | | | | | |
| | WK2 | | | | | | | |
| | WK3 | | | | | | | |
| | WK4 | | | | | | | |

ENGAGEMENT ACTIVITY:

| | | SUN | MON | TUE | WED | THU | FRI | SAT |
|---|---|---|---|---|---|---|---|---|
| NOTES: | WK1 | | | | | | | |
| | WK2 | | | | | | | |
| | WK3 | | | | | | | |
| | WK4 | | | | | | | |

# April 2026

6 MONDAY

7 TUESDAY

8 WEDNESDAY

National All Is Ours Day

NOTES

9 THURSDAY

10 FRIDAY

11 SATURDAY

12 SUNDAY

# April 2026

## TOP TO-DOS THIS WEEK

- [ ] 
- [ ] 
- [ ] 
- [ ] 
- [ ] 
- [ ] 

## FOLLOW UPS

## APPOINTMENTS

MON

TUE

WED

THU

FRI

SAT

SUN

## SOCIAL MEDIA FOCUS/GOAL THIS WEEK

Creativity is your superpower. Use it like it pays the bills.

## SOCIAL MEDIA ENGAGEMENT PLAN & TRACKER

ENGAGEMENT ACTIVITY:

| | | SUN | MON | TUE | WED | THU | FRI | SAT |
|---|---|---|---|---|---|---|---|---|
| NOTES: | WK1 | | | | | | | |
| | WK2 | | | | | | | |
| | WK3 | | | | | | | |
| | WK4 | | | | | | | |

ENGAGEMENT ACTIVITY:

| | | SUN | MON | TUE | WED | THU | FRI | SAT |
|---|---|---|---|---|---|---|---|---|
| NOTES: | WK1 | | | | | | | |
| | WK2 | | | | | | | |
| | WK3 | | | | | | | |
| | WK4 | | | | | | | |

ENGAGEMENT ACTIVITY:

| | | SUN | MON | TUE | WED | THU | FRI | SAT |
|---|---|---|---|---|---|---|---|---|
| NOTES: | WK1 | | | | | | | |
| | WK2 | | | | | | | |
| | WK3 | | | | | | | |
| | WK4 | | | | | | | |

ENGAGEMENT ACTIVITY:

| | | SUN | MON | TUE | WED | THU | FRI | SAT |
|---|---|---|---|---|---|---|---|---|
| NOTES: | WK1 | | | | | | | |
| | WK2 | | | | | | | |
| | WK3 | | | | | | | |
| | WK4 | | | | | | | |

ENGAGEMENT ACTIVITY:

| | | SUN | MON | TUE | WED | THU | FRI | SAT |
|---|---|---|---|---|---|---|---|---|
| NOTES: | WK1 | | | | | | | |
| | WK2 | | | | | | | |
| | WK3 | | | | | | | |
| | WK4 | | | | | | | |

# April 2026

## 13 MONDAY

## 14 TUESDAY

## 15 WEDNESDAY

National Tax Day

NOTES

16 THURSDAY

17 FRIDAY

18 SATURDAY

19 SUNDAY

# April 2026

## TOP TO-DOS THIS WEEK

## FOLLOW UPS

## APPOINTMENTS

MON

TUE

WED

THU

FRI

SAT

SUN

## SOCIAL MEDIA FOCUS/GOAL THIS WEEK

Create first. Confidence follows.

# SOCIAL MEDIA ENGAGEMENT PLAN & TRACKER

ENGAGEMENT ACTIVITY:

| | | SUN | MON | TUE | WED | THU | FRI | SAT |
|---|---|---|---|---|---|---|---|---|
| NOTES: | WK1 | | | | | | | |
| | WK2 | | | | | | | |
| | WK3 | | | | | | | |
| | WK4 | | | | | | | |

ENGAGEMENT ACTIVITY:

| | | SUN | MON | TUE | WED | THU | FRI | SAT |
|---|---|---|---|---|---|---|---|---|
| NOTES: | WK1 | | | | | | | |
| | WK2 | | | | | | | |
| | WK3 | | | | | | | |
| | WK4 | | | | | | | |

ENGAGEMENT ACTIVITY:

| | | SUN | MON | TUE | WED | THU | FRI | SAT |
|---|---|---|---|---|---|---|---|---|
| NOTES: | WK1 | | | | | | | |
| | WK2 | | | | | | | |
| | WK3 | | | | | | | |
| | WK4 | | | | | | | |

ENGAGEMENT ACTIVITY:

| | | SUN | MON | TUE | WED | THU | FRI | SAT |
|---|---|---|---|---|---|---|---|---|
| NOTES: | WK1 | | | | | | | |
| | WK2 | | | | | | | |
| | WK3 | | | | | | | |
| | WK4 | | | | | | | |

ENGAGEMENT ACTIVITY:

| | | SUN | MON | TUE | WED | THU | FRI | SAT |
|---|---|---|---|---|---|---|---|---|
| NOTES: | WK1 | | | | | | | |
| | WK2 | | | | | | | |
| | WK3 | | | | | | | |
| | WK4 | | | | | | | |

# April 2026

20 MONDAY

21 TUESDAY

22 WEDNESDAY

Earth Day

NOTES

23 THURSDAY

National Take a Chance Day

24 FRIDAY

25 SATURDAY

26 SUNDAY

# April 2026

## TOP TO-DOS THIS WEEK

- [ ] 
- [ ] 
- [ ] 
- [ ] 
- [ ] 
- [ ] 

## FOLLOW UPS

## APPOINTMENTS

MON

TUE

WED

THU

FRI

SAT

SUN

## SOCIAL MEDIA FOCUS/GOAL THIS WEEK

Done with doubt – full speed ahead!

# SOCIAL MEDIA ENGAGEMENT PLAN & TRACKER

ENGAGEMENT ACTIVITY:

| | | SUN | MON | TUE | WED | THU | FRI | SAT |
|---|---|---|---|---|---|---|---|---|
| NOTES: | WK1 | | | | | | | |
| | WK2 | | | | | | | |
| | WK3 | | | | | | | |
| | WK4 | | | | | | | |

ENGAGEMENT ACTIVITY:

| | | SUN | MON | TUE | WED | THU | FRI | SAT |
|---|---|---|---|---|---|---|---|---|
| NOTES: | WK1 | | | | | | | |
| | WK2 | | | | | | | |
| | WK3 | | | | | | | |
| | WK4 | | | | | | | |

ENGAGEMENT ACTIVITY:

| | | SUN | MON | TUE | WED | THU | FRI | SAT |
|---|---|---|---|---|---|---|---|---|
| NOTES: | WK1 | | | | | | | |
| | WK2 | | | | | | | |
| | WK3 | | | | | | | |
| | WK4 | | | | | | | |

ENGAGEMENT ACTIVITY:

| | | SUN | MON | TUE | WED | THU | FRI | SAT |
|---|---|---|---|---|---|---|---|---|
| NOTES: | WK1 | | | | | | | |
| | WK2 | | | | | | | |
| | WK3 | | | | | | | |
| | WK4 | | | | | | | |

ENGAGEMENT ACTIVITY:

| | | SUN | MON | TUE | WED | THU | FRI | SAT |
|---|---|---|---|---|---|---|---|---|
| NOTES: | WK1 | | | | | | | |
| | WK2 | | | | | | | |
| | WK3 | | | | | | | |
| | WK4 | | | | | | | |

# April 2026

27 MONDAY

28 TUESDAY

29 WEDNESDAY

NOTES

30 THURSDAY

1 FRIDAY

May Day

2 SATURDAY

3 SUNDAY

# April 2026

## MONTH IN REVIEW

### I AM GRATEFUL FOR

### CONNECTED WITH

### PERSONAL WINS

### WHAT I LEARNED

### GOALS MET

### PREFERED PLATFORM GROWTH

### TOP PERFORMING POST

**Doers — spring it on: what clicked for you this month?**
**Share in the Plandipity Doer's Inner Circle (Our Private FB Group)**

"PINK IS THE COLOR OF STRENGTH,

*a color of conviction,*

A COLOR OF DECISION-MAKING."

**ANGAD BEDI.**

# *May* 2026

# May 2026

## Business Goal

What's the one thing that will move your business forward this month?

## Personal Goal

What personal win or habit will make life easier or happier?

## Social Media Marketing Planning

### KEY DATES

What holidays, launches, or community events should you post about?

### THIS MONTH'S MARKETING FOCUS

### BUSINESS EVENTS

### PERSONAL EVENTS

PLAN WITH ME!

Grab your favorite drink and let's brainstorm together.
Scan the QR code to plan your May content with me!

# My Tasks This Month

NOTES AND IDEAS

Ready for a little momentum boost?
Scan to see everything coming up - free webinars, live trainings, and helpful downloads all in one easy place.

# May 2026

| SUNDAY | MONDAY | TUESDAY | WEDNESDAY |
|---|---|---|---|
| 26 | 27 | 28 | 29 |
| 3 | 4 | 5 | 6 |
| 10 | 11 | 12 | 13 |
| 17 | 18 | 19 | 20 |
| 24 | 25 | 26 | 27 |

| THURSDAY | FRIDAY | SATURDAY |
|---|---|---|
| 30 | 1 | 2 |
| 7 | 8 | 9 |
| 14 | 15 | 16<br>CONTENT CABOODLE DROPS TODAY! |
| 21 | 22 | 23 |
| 28 | 29 | 30 |

## Notes

## Reminders

**Doer's: be sure to register for weekly We Plan Wednesdays**

# May 2026

## TOP TO-DOS THIS WEEK

## FOLLOW UPS

## APPOINTMENTS

MON

TUE

WED

THU

FRI

SAT

SUN

## SOCIAL MEDIA FOCUS/GOAL THIS WEEK

You already know
what to do
- trust yourself!

# SOCIAL MEDIA ENGAGEMENT PLAN & TRACKER

ENGAGEMENT ACTIVITY:

| | | SUN | MON | TUE | WED | THU | FRI | SAT |
|---|---|---|---|---|---|---|---|---|
| NOTES: | WK1 | | | | | | | |
| | WK2 | | | | | | | |
| | WK3 | | | | | | | |
| | WK4 | | | | | | | |

ENGAGEMENT ACTIVITY:

| | | SUN | MON | TUE | WED | THU | FRI | SAT |
|---|---|---|---|---|---|---|---|---|
| NOTES: | WK1 | | | | | | | |
| | WK2 | | | | | | | |
| | WK3 | | | | | | | |
| | WK4 | | | | | | | |

ENGAGEMENT ACTIVITY:

| | | SUN | MON | TUE | WED | THU | FRI | SAT |
|---|---|---|---|---|---|---|---|---|
| NOTES: | WK1 | | | | | | | |
| | WK2 | | | | | | | |
| | WK3 | | | | | | | |
| | WK4 | | | | | | | |

ENGAGEMENT ACTIVITY:

| | | SUN | MON | TUE | WED | THU | FRI | SAT |
|---|---|---|---|---|---|---|---|---|
| NOTES: | WK1 | | | | | | | |
| | WK2 | | | | | | | |
| | WK3 | | | | | | | |
| | WK4 | | | | | | | |

ENGAGEMENT ACTIVITY:

| | | SUN | MON | TUE | WED | THU | FRI | SAT |
|---|---|---|---|---|---|---|---|---|
| NOTES: | WK1 | | | | | | | |
| | WK2 | | | | | | | |
| | WK3 | | | | | | | |
| | WK4 | | | | | | | |

# May 2026

4 MONDAY

May The $4^{TH}$ Be With You - Star Wars Day

5 TUESDAY

Cinco de Mayo

6 WEDNESDAY

NOTES

7 THURSDAY

8 FRIDAY

9 SATURDAY

10 SUNDAY

# May 2026

## TOP TO-DOS THIS WEEK

## FOLLOW UPS

## APPOINTMENTS

MON

TUE

WED

THU

FRI

SAT

SUN

## SOCIAL MEDIA FOCUS/GOAL THIS WEEK

Let your work *shine* as bright as your *heart!*

# SOCIAL MEDIA ENGAGEMENT PLAN & TRACKER

ENGAGEMENT ACTIVITY:

| | | SUN | MON | TUE | WED | THU | FRI | SAT |
|---|---|---|---|---|---|---|---|---|
| NOTES: | WK1 | | | | | | | |
| | WK2 | | | | | | | |
| | WK3 | | | | | | | |
| | WK4 | | | | | | | |

ENGAGEMENT ACTIVITY:

| | | SUN | MON | TUE | WED | THU | FRI | SAT |
|---|---|---|---|---|---|---|---|---|
| NOTES: | WK1 | | | | | | | |
| | WK2 | | | | | | | |
| | WK3 | | | | | | | |
| | WK4 | | | | | | | |

ENGAGEMENT ACTIVITY:

| | | SUN | MON | TUE | WED | THU | FRI | SAT |
|---|---|---|---|---|---|---|---|---|
| NOTES: | WK1 | | | | | | | |
| | WK2 | | | | | | | |
| | WK3 | | | | | | | |
| | WK4 | | | | | | | |

ENGAGEMENT ACTIVITY:

| | | SUN | MON | TUE | WED | THU | FRI | SAT |
|---|---|---|---|---|---|---|---|---|
| NOTES: | WK1 | | | | | | | |
| | WK2 | | | | | | | |
| | WK3 | | | | | | | |
| | WK4 | | | | | | | |

ENGAGEMENT ACTIVITY:

| | | SUN | MON | TUE | WED | THU | FRI | SAT |
|---|---|---|---|---|---|---|---|---|
| NOTES: | WK1 | | | | | | | |
| | WK2 | | | | | | | |
| | WK3 | | | | | | | |
| | WK4 | | | | | | | |

# May 2026

11 MONDAY

12 TUESDAY

National Teacher Appreciation Day

13 WEDNESDAY

NOTES

14 THURSDAY

15 FRIDAY

16 SATURDAY

17 SUNDAY

# May 2026

## TOP TO-DOS THIS WEEK

## FOLLOW UPS

## APPOINTMENTS

MON

TUE

WED

THU

FRI

SAT

SUN

## SOCIAL MEDIA FOCUS/GOAL THIS WEEK

Clarity doesn't come first, decisions do.

# SOCIAL MEDIA ENGAGEMENT PLAN & TRACKER

ENGAGEMENT ACTIVITY:

| | | SUN | MON | TUE | WED | THU | FRI | SAT |
|---|---|---|---|---|---|---|---|---|
| NOTES: | WK1 | | | | | | | |
| | WK2 | | | | | | | |
| | WK3 | | | | | | | |
| | WK4 | | | | | | | |

ENGAGEMENT ACTIVITY:

| | | SUN | MON | TUE | WED | THU | FRI | SAT |
|---|---|---|---|---|---|---|---|---|
| NOTES: | WK1 | | | | | | | |
| | WK2 | | | | | | | |
| | WK3 | | | | | | | |
| | WK4 | | | | | | | |

ENGAGEMENT ACTIVITY:

| | | SUN | MON | TUE | WED | THU | FRI | SAT |
|---|---|---|---|---|---|---|---|---|
| NOTES: | WK1 | | | | | | | |
| | WK2 | | | | | | | |
| | WK3 | | | | | | | |
| | WK4 | | | | | | | |

ENGAGEMENT ACTIVITY:

| | | SUN | MON | TUE | WED | THU | FRI | SAT |
|---|---|---|---|---|---|---|---|---|
| NOTES: | WK1 | | | | | | | |
| | WK2 | | | | | | | |
| | WK3 | | | | | | | |
| | WK4 | | | | | | | |

ENGAGEMENT ACTIVITY:

| | | SUN | MON | TUE | WED | THU | FRI | SAT |
|---|---|---|---|---|---|---|---|---|
| NOTES: | WK1 | | | | | | | |
| | WK2 | | | | | | | |
| | WK3 | | | | | | | |
| | WK4 | | | | | | | |

# May 2026

18 MONDAY

19 TUESDAY

20 WEDNESDAY

NOTES

21 THURSDAY

22 FRIDAY

23 SATURDAY

24 SUNDAY

# May 2026

## TOP TO-DOS THIS WEEK

## FOLLOW UPS

## APPOINTMENTS

MON

TUE

WED

THU

FRI

SAT

SUN

## SOCIAL MEDIA FOCUS/GOAL THIS WEEK

Own your energy, own your outcomes!

# SOCIAL MEDIA ENGAGEMENT PLAN & TRACKER

ENGAGEMENT ACTIVITY:

| | | SUN | MON | TUE | WED | THU | FRI | SAT |
|---|---|---|---|---|---|---|---|---|
| NOTES: | WK1 | | | | | | | |
| | WK2 | | | | | | | |
| | WK3 | | | | | | | |
| | WK4 | | | | | | | |

ENGAGEMENT ACTIVITY:

| | | SUN | MON | TUE | WED | THU | FRI | SAT |
|---|---|---|---|---|---|---|---|---|
| NOTES: | WK1 | | | | | | | |
| | WK2 | | | | | | | |
| | WK3 | | | | | | | |
| | WK4 | | | | | | | |

ENGAGEMENT ACTIVITY:

| | | SUN | MON | TUE | WED | THU | FRI | SAT |
|---|---|---|---|---|---|---|---|---|
| NOTES: | WK1 | | | | | | | |
| | WK2 | | | | | | | |
| | WK3 | | | | | | | |
| | WK4 | | | | | | | |

ENGAGEMENT ACTIVITY:

| | | SUN | MON | TUE | WED | THU | FRI | SAT |
|---|---|---|---|---|---|---|---|---|
| NOTES: | WK1 | | | | | | | |
| | WK2 | | | | | | | |
| | WK3 | | | | | | | |
| | WK4 | | | | | | | |

ENGAGEMENT ACTIVITY:

| | | SUN | MON | TUE | WED | THU | FRI | SAT |
|---|---|---|---|---|---|---|---|---|
| NOTES: | WK1 | | | | | | | |
| | WK2 | | | | | | | |
| | WK3 | | | | | | | |
| | WK4 | | | | | | | |

# May 2026

25 MONDAY

Memorial Day

26 TUESDAY

27 WEDNESDAY

NOTES

28 THURSDAY

29 FRIDAY

30 SATURDAY

National Creativity Day

31 SUNDAY

# May 2026

## MONTH IN REVIEW

### I AM GRATEFUL FOR

### CONNECTED WITH

### PERSONAL WINS

### WHAT I LEARNED

### GOALS MET

### PREFERED PLATFORM GROWTH

### TOP PERFORMING POST

Doers — May we brag on you? Share a win or a-ha in the Plandipity Doer's Inner Circle (Our Private FB Group)

"YOUR CAN'T *move mountains* BY WHISPERING AT THEM."

P!NK

# *June* 2026

# June 2026

## Business Goal

What's the one thing that will move your business forward this month?

## Personal Goal

What personal win or habit will make life easier or happier?

## Social Media Marketing Planning

### KEY DATES

What holidays, launches, or community events should you post about?

- 
- 
- 
- 
- 

### THIS MONTH'S MARKETING FOCUS

### BUSINESS EVENTS

### PERSONAL EVENTS

PLAN WITH ME!

**Midyear reset time! Scan the QR code and let's plan your content for a confident, consistent June.**

# My Tasks This Month

NOTES AND IDEAS

Mid-year check-in! Surround yourself with people who'll keep you accountable and inspired.

Become a Doer and stay consistent!

# June 2026

| SUNDAY | MONDAY | TUESDAY | WEDNESDAY |
|---|---|---|---|
| 31 | 1 | 2 | 3 |
| 7 | 8 | 9 | 10 |
| 14 | 15 | 16 | 17 |
| 21 | 22 | 23 | 24 |
| 28 | 29 | 30 | 1 |

| THURSDAY | FRIDAY | SATURDAY |
| --- | --- | --- |
| 4 | 5 | 6 |
| 11 | 12 | 13 |
| 18 | 19 | 20<br>CONTENT CABOODLE DROPS TODAY! |
| 25 | 26 | 27 |
| 2 | 3 | 4 |

Notes

Reminders

**Doer's: be sure to register for weekly We Plan Wednesdays**

# June 2026

## TOP TO-DOS THIS WEEK

## FOLLOW UPS

## APPOINTMENTS

MON

TUE

WED

THU

FRI

SAT

SUN

## SOCIAL MEDIA FOCUS/GOAL THIS WEEK

You are the CEO of your confidence!

# SOCIAL MEDIA ENGAGEMENT PLAN & TRACKER

ENGAGEMENT ACTIVITY:

| | | SUN | MON | TUE | WED | THU | FRI | SAT |
|---|---|---|---|---|---|---|---|---|
| NOTES: | WK1 | | | | | | | |
| | WK2 | | | | | | | |
| | WK3 | | | | | | | |
| | WK4 | | | | | | | |

ENGAGEMENT ACTIVITY:

| | | SUN | MON | TUE | WED | THU | FRI | SAT |
|---|---|---|---|---|---|---|---|---|
| NOTES: | WK1 | | | | | | | |
| | WK2 | | | | | | | |
| | WK3 | | | | | | | |
| | WK4 | | | | | | | |

ENGAGEMENT ACTIVITY:

| | | SUN | MON | TUE | WED | THU | FRI | SAT |
|---|---|---|---|---|---|---|---|---|
| NOTES: | WK1 | | | | | | | |
| | WK2 | | | | | | | |
| | WK3 | | | | | | | |
| | WK4 | | | | | | | |

ENGAGEMENT ACTIVITY:

| | | SUN | MON | TUE | WED | THU | FRI | SAT |
|---|---|---|---|---|---|---|---|---|
| NOTES: | WK1 | | | | | | | |
| | WK2 | | | | | | | |
| | WK3 | | | | | | | |
| | WK4 | | | | | | | |

ENGAGEMENT ACTIVITY:

| | | SUN | MON | TUE | WED | THU | FRI | SAT |
|---|---|---|---|---|---|---|---|---|
| NOTES: | WK1 | | | | | | | |
| | WK2 | | | | | | | |
| | WK3 | | | | | | | |
| | WK4 | | | | | | | |

# June 2026

1 MONDAY

2 TUESDAY

National Leave the Office Early Day

3 WEDNESDAY

NOTES

4 THURSDAY

5 FRIDAY

6 SATURDAY

7 SUNDAY

# June 2026

## TOP TO-DOS THIS WEEK

- [ ] 
- [ ] 
- [ ] 
- [ ] 
- [ ] 
- [ ] 

## FOLLOW UPS

## APPOINTMENTS

MON

TUE

WED

THU

FRI

SAT

SUN

## SOCIAL MEDIA FOCUS/GOAL THIS WEEK

Show up like you mean it!

# SOCIAL MEDIA ENGAGEMENT PLAN & TRACKER

ENGAGEMENT ACTIVITY:

| | | SUN | MON | TUE | WED | THU | FRI | SAT |
|---|---|---|---|---|---|---|---|---|
| NOTES: | WK1 | | | | | | | |
| | WK2 | | | | | | | |
| | WK3 | | | | | | | |
| | WK4 | | | | | | | |

ENGAGEMENT ACTIVITY:

| | | SUN | MON | TUE | WED | THU | FRI | SAT |
|---|---|---|---|---|---|---|---|---|
| NOTES: | WK1 | | | | | | | |
| | WK2 | | | | | | | |
| | WK3 | | | | | | | |
| | WK4 | | | | | | | |

ENGAGEMENT ACTIVITY:

| | | SUN | MON | TUE | WED | THU | FRI | SAT |
|---|---|---|---|---|---|---|---|---|
| NOTES: | WK1 | | | | | | | |
| | WK2 | | | | | | | |
| | WK3 | | | | | | | |
| | WK4 | | | | | | | |

ENGAGEMENT ACTIVITY:

| | | SUN | MON | TUE | WED | THU | FRI | SAT |
|---|---|---|---|---|---|---|---|---|
| NOTES: | WK1 | | | | | | | |
| | WK2 | | | | | | | |
| | WK3 | | | | | | | |
| | WK4 | | | | | | | |

ENGAGEMENT ACTIVITY:

| | | SUN | MON | TUE | WED | THU | FRI | SAT |
|---|---|---|---|---|---|---|---|---|
| NOTES: | WK1 | | | | | | | |
| | WK2 | | | | | | | |
| | WK3 | | | | | | | |
| | WK4 | | | | | | | |

# June 2026

8 MONDAY

9 TUESDAY

10 WEDNESDAY

NOTES

11 THURSDAY

12 FRIDAY

13 SATURDAY

14 SUNDAY

# June 2026

## TOP TO-DOS THIS WEEK

- [ ]
- [ ]
- [ ]
- [ ]
- [ ]
- [ ]

## FOLLOW UPS

## APPOINTMENTS

MON

TUE

WED

THU

FRI

SAT

SUN

## SOCIAL MEDIA FOCUS/GOAL THIS WEEK

Growth feels awkward before it feels right.

# SOCIAL MEDIA ENGAGEMENT PLAN & TRACKER

ENGAGEMENT ACTIVITY:

| | | SUN | MON | TUE | WED | THU | FRI | SAT |
|---|---|---|---|---|---|---|---|---|
| NOTES: | WK1 | | | | | | | |
| | WK2 | | | | | | | |
| | WK3 | | | | | | | |
| | WK4 | | | | | | | |

ENGAGEMENT ACTIVITY:

| | | SUN | MON | TUE | WED | THU | FRI | SAT |
|---|---|---|---|---|---|---|---|---|
| NOTES: | WK1 | | | | | | | |
| | WK2 | | | | | | | |
| | WK3 | | | | | | | |
| | WK4 | | | | | | | |

ENGAGEMENT ACTIVITY:

| | | SUN | MON | TUE | WED | THU | FRI | SAT |
|---|---|---|---|---|---|---|---|---|
| NOTES: | WK1 | | | | | | | |
| | WK2 | | | | | | | |
| | WK3 | | | | | | | |
| | WK4 | | | | | | | |

ENGAGEMENT ACTIVITY:

| | | SUN | MON | TUE | WED | THU | FRI | SAT |
|---|---|---|---|---|---|---|---|---|
| NOTES: | WK1 | | | | | | | |
| | WK2 | | | | | | | |
| | WK3 | | | | | | | |
| | WK4 | | | | | | | |

ENGAGEMENT ACTIVITY:

| | | SUN | MON | TUE | WED | THU | FRI | SAT |
|---|---|---|---|---|---|---|---|---|
| NOTES: | WK1 | | | | | | | |
| | WK2 | | | | | | | |
| | WK3 | | | | | | | |
| | WK4 | | | | | | | |

# June 2026

15 MONDAY

16 TUESDAY

17 WEDNESDAY

NOTES

18 THURSDAY

19 FRIDAY

Juneteenth National Independence Day

20 SATURDAY

First Day of Summer

21 SUNDAY

Father's day

National Selfie Day

# June 2026

## TOP TO-DOS THIS WEEK

- [ ]
- [ ]
- [ ]
- [ ]
- [ ]
- [ ]

## FOLLOW UPS

## APPOINTMENTS

**MON**

**TUE**

**WED**

**THU**

**FRI**

**SAT**

**SUN**

## SOCIAL MEDIA FOCUS/GOAL THIS WEEK

Crown on.
Chin up.
You've got
queen energy.

# SOCIAL MEDIA ENGAGEMENT PLAN & TRACKER

ENGAGEMENT ACTIVITY:

| | | SUN | MON | TUE | WED | THU | FRI | SAT |
|---|---|---|---|---|---|---|---|---|
| NOTES: | WK1 | | | | | | | |
| | WK2 | | | | | | | |
| | WK3 | | | | | | | |
| | WK4 | | | | | | | |

ENGAGEMENT ACTIVITY:

| | | SUN | MON | TUE | WED | THU | FRI | SAT |
|---|---|---|---|---|---|---|---|---|
| NOTES: | WK1 | | | | | | | |
| | WK2 | | | | | | | |
| | WK3 | | | | | | | |
| | WK4 | | | | | | | |

ENGAGEMENT ACTIVITY:

| | | SUN | MON | TUE | WED | THU | FRI | SAT |
|---|---|---|---|---|---|---|---|---|
| NOTES: | WK1 | | | | | | | |
| | WK2 | | | | | | | |
| | WK3 | | | | | | | |
| | WK4 | | | | | | | |

ENGAGEMENT ACTIVITY:

| | | SUN | MON | TUE | WED | THU | FRI | SAT |
|---|---|---|---|---|---|---|---|---|
| NOTES: | WK1 | | | | | | | |
| | WK2 | | | | | | | |
| | WK3 | | | | | | | |
| | WK4 | | | | | | | |

ENGAGEMENT ACTIVITY:

| | | SUN | MON | TUE | WED | THU | FRI | SAT |
|---|---|---|---|---|---|---|---|---|
| NOTES: | WK1 | | | | | | | |
| | WK2 | | | | | | | |
| | WK3 | | | | | | | |
| | WK4 | | | | | | | |

# June 2026

22 MONDAY

23 TUESDAY

24 WEDNESDAY

NOTES

25 THURSDAY

26 FRIDAY

27 SATURDAY

28 SUNDAY

# June 2026

## TOP TO-DOS THIS WEEK

- [ ] 
- [ ] 
- [ ] 
- [ ] 
- [ ] 
- [ ] 

## FOLLOW UPS

## APPOINTMENTS

MON

TUE

WED

THU

FRI

SAT

SUN

## SOCIAL MEDIA FOCUS/GOAL THIS WEEK

Shine with purpose!

# SOCIAL MEDIA ENGAGEMENT PLAN & TRACKER

ENGAGEMENT ACTIVITY:

| | | SUN | MON | TUE | WED | THU | FRI | SAT |
|---|---|---|---|---|---|---|---|---|
| NOTES: | WK1 | | | | | | | |
| | WK2 | | | | | | | |
| | WK3 | | | | | | | |
| | WK4 | | | | | | | |

ENGAGEMENT ACTIVITY:

| | | SUN | MON | TUE | WED | THU | FRI | SAT |
|---|---|---|---|---|---|---|---|---|
| NOTES: | WK1 | | | | | | | |
| | WK2 | | | | | | | |
| | WK3 | | | | | | | |
| | WK4 | | | | | | | |

ENGAGEMENT ACTIVITY:

| | | SUN | MON | TUE | WED | THU | FRI | SAT |
|---|---|---|---|---|---|---|---|---|
| NOTES: | WK1 | | | | | | | |
| | WK2 | | | | | | | |
| | WK3 | | | | | | | |
| | WK4 | | | | | | | |

ENGAGEMENT ACTIVITY:

| | | SUN | MON | TUE | WED | THU | FRI | SAT |
|---|---|---|---|---|---|---|---|---|
| NOTES: | WK1 | | | | | | | |
| | WK2 | | | | | | | |
| | WK3 | | | | | | | |
| | WK4 | | | | | | | |

ENGAGEMENT ACTIVITY:

| | | SUN | MON | TUE | WED | THU | FRI | SAT |
|---|---|---|---|---|---|---|---|---|
| NOTES: | WK1 | | | | | | | |
| | WK2 | | | | | | | |
| | WK3 | | | | | | | |
| | WK4 | | | | | | | |

# June 2026

29 MONDAY

30 TUESDAY Social Media Day

1 WEDNESDAY

NOTES

2 THURSDAY

3 FRIDAY

4 SATURDAY

Independence Day

5 SUNDAY

National Workaholics Day

# June 2026

## MONTH IN REVIEW

I AM GRATEFUL FOR

CONNECTED WITH

PERSONAL WINS

WHAT I LEARNED

GOALS MET

PREFERED PLATFORM GROWTH

TOP PERFORMING POST

Doers — midyear magic: post your biggest June insight in the Plandipity Doer's Inner Circle (Our Private FB Group)

"DON'T JUST DREAM IT

*Be it!*

**SUSAN BOYLE**

# July 2026

# July 2026

## Business Goal

What's the one thing that will move your business forward this month?

## Personal Goal

What personal win or habit will make life easier or happier?

## Social Media Marketing Planning

### KEY DATES

What holidays, launches, or community events should you post about?

- ______________________________
- ______________________________
- ______________________________
- ______________________________
- ______________________________

### THIS MONTH'S MARKETING FOCUS

### BUSINESS EVENTS

### PERSONAL EVENTS

**Summer vibes, steady growth. Scan the QR code to plan July's content and keep your strategy shining.**

# My Tasks This Month

NOTES AND IDEAS

# July 2026

| SUNDAY | MONDAY | TUESDAY | WEDNESDAY |
| --- | --- | --- | --- |
| 28 | 29 | 30 | 1 |
| 5 | 6 | 7 | 8 |
| 12 | 13 | 14 | 15 |
| 19 | 20 | 21 | 22 |
| 26 | 27 | 28 | 29 |

| THURSDAY | FRIDAY | SATURDAY |
| --- | --- | --- |
| 2 | 3 | 4 |
| 9 | 10 | 11 |
| 16 | 17 | 18<br>CONTENT CABOODLE DROPS TODAY! |
| 23 | 24 | 25 |
| 30 | 31 | 1 |

Notes

Reminders

Doer's: be sure to register for weekly We Plan Wednesdays

# July 2026

## TOP TO-DOS THIS WEEK

- [ ] 
- [ ] 
- [ ] 
- [ ] 
- [ ] 
- [ ] 

## FOLLOW UPS

## APPOINTMENTS

MON

TUE

WED

THU

FRI

SAT

SUN

## SOCIAL MEDIA FOCUS/GOAL THIS WEEK

Imperfect action beats perfect hesitation.

## SOCIAL MEDIA ENGAGEMENT PLAN & TRACKER

ENGAGEMENT ACTIVITY:

| | | SUN | MON | TUE | WED | THU | FRI | SAT |
|---|---|---|---|---|---|---|---|---|
| NOTES: | WK1 | | | | | | | |
| | WK2 | | | | | | | |
| | WK3 | | | | | | | |
| | WK4 | | | | | | | |

ENGAGEMENT ACTIVITY:

| | | SUN | MON | TUE | WED | THU | FRI | SAT |
|---|---|---|---|---|---|---|---|---|
| NOTES: | WK1 | | | | | | | |
| | WK2 | | | | | | | |
| | WK3 | | | | | | | |
| | WK4 | | | | | | | |

ENGAGEMENT ACTIVITY:

| | | SUN | MON | TUE | WED | THU | FRI | SAT |
|---|---|---|---|---|---|---|---|---|
| NOTES: | WK1 | | | | | | | |
| | WK2 | | | | | | | |
| | WK3 | | | | | | | |
| | WK4 | | | | | | | |

ENGAGEMENT ACTIVITY:

| | | SUN | MON | TUE | WED | THU | FRI | SAT |
|---|---|---|---|---|---|---|---|---|
| NOTES: | WK1 | | | | | | | |
| | WK2 | | | | | | | |
| | WK3 | | | | | | | |
| | WK4 | | | | | | | |

ENGAGEMENT ACTIVITY:

| | | SUN | MON | TUE | WED | THU | FRI | SAT |
|---|---|---|---|---|---|---|---|---|
| NOTES: | WK1 | | | | | | | |
| | WK2 | | | | | | | |
| | WK3 | | | | | | | |
| | WK4 | | | | | | | |

# July 2026

6 MONDAY

7 TUESDAY

8 WEDNESDAY

NOTES

9 THURSDAY

10 FRIDAY

11 SATURDAY

National Simplicity Day

12 SUNDAY

# July 2026

## TOP TO-DOS THIS WEEK

## FOLLOW UPS

## APPOINTMENTS

MON

TUE

WED

THU

FRI

SAT

SUN

## SOCIAL MEDIA FOCUS/GOAL THIS WEEK

Mistakes?
Proof you're
doing the damn
thing.

## SOCIAL MEDIA ENGAGEMENT PLAN & TRACKER

ENGAGEMENT ACTIVITY:

| | | SUN | MON | TUE | WED | THU | FRI | SAT |
|---|---|---|---|---|---|---|---|---|
| NOTES: | WK1 | | | | | | | |
| | WK2 | | | | | | | |
| | WK3 | | | | | | | |
| | WK4 | | | | | | | |

ENGAGEMENT ACTIVITY:

| | | SUN | MON | TUE | WED | THU | FRI | SAT |
|---|---|---|---|---|---|---|---|---|
| NOTES: | WK1 | | | | | | | |
| | WK2 | | | | | | | |
| | WK3 | | | | | | | |
| | WK4 | | | | | | | |

ENGAGEMENT ACTIVITY:

| | | SUN | MON | TUE | WED | THU | FRI | SAT |
|---|---|---|---|---|---|---|---|---|
| NOTES: | WK1 | | | | | | | |
| | WK2 | | | | | | | |
| | WK3 | | | | | | | |
| | WK4 | | | | | | | |

ENGAGEMENT ACTIVITY:

| | | SUN | MON | TUE | WED | THU | FRI | SAT |
|---|---|---|---|---|---|---|---|---|
| NOTES: | WK1 | | | | | | | |
| | WK2 | | | | | | | |
| | WK3 | | | | | | | |
| | WK4 | | | | | | | |

ENGAGEMENT ACTIVITY:

| | | SUN | MON | TUE | WED | THU | FRI | SAT |
|---|---|---|---|---|---|---|---|---|
| NOTES: | WK1 | | | | | | | |
| | WK2 | | | | | | | |
| | WK3 | | | | | | | |
| | WK4 | | | | | | | |

# July 2026

13 MONDAY

14 TUESDAY

15 WEDNESDAY

NOTES

16 THURSDAY

Get to Know Your Customers Day

Third Thursday of each Quarter

17 FRIDAY

18 SATURDAY

19 SUNDAY

# July 2026

## TOP TO-DOS THIS WEEK

- [ ] 
- [ ] 
- [ ] 
- [ ] 
- [ ] 
- [ ] 

## FOLLOW UPS

## APPOINTMENTS

MON

TUE

WED

THU

FRI

SAT

SUN

## SOCIAL MEDIA FOCUS/GOAL THIS WEEK

You don't need permission to *shine.* Just light the match.

# SOCIAL MEDIA ENGAGEMENT PLAN & TRACKER

ENGAGEMENT ACTIVITY:

| | | SUN | MON | TUE | WED | THU | FRI | SAT |
|---|---|---|---|---|---|---|---|---|
| NOTES: | WK1 | | | | | | | |
| | WK2 | | | | | | | |
| | WK3 | | | | | | | |
| | WK4 | | | | | | | |

ENGAGEMENT ACTIVITY:

| | | SUN | MON | TUE | WED | THU | FRI | SAT |
|---|---|---|---|---|---|---|---|---|
| NOTES: | WK1 | | | | | | | |
| | WK2 | | | | | | | |
| | WK3 | | | | | | | |
| | WK4 | | | | | | | |

ENGAGEMENT ACTIVITY:

| | | SUN | MON | TUE | WED | THU | FRI | SAT |
|---|---|---|---|---|---|---|---|---|
| NOTES: | WK1 | | | | | | | |
| | WK2 | | | | | | | |
| | WK3 | | | | | | | |
| | WK4 | | | | | | | |

ENGAGEMENT ACTIVITY:

| | | SUN | MON | TUE | WED | THU | FRI | SAT |
|---|---|---|---|---|---|---|---|---|
| NOTES: | WK1 | | | | | | | |
| | WK2 | | | | | | | |
| | WK3 | | | | | | | |
| | WK4 | | | | | | | |

ENGAGEMENT ACTIVITY:

| | | SUN | MON | TUE | WED | THU | FRI | SAT |
|---|---|---|---|---|---|---|---|---|
| NOTES: | WK1 | | | | | | | |
| | WK2 | | | | | | | |
| | WK3 | | | | | | | |
| | WK4 | | | | | | | |

# July 2026

20 MONDAY

21 TUESDAY

22 WEDNESDAY

NOTES

23 THURSDAY

24 FRIDAY

25 SATURDAY

26 SUNDAY

# July 2026

## TOP TO-DOS THIS WEEK

- [ ] 
- [ ] 
- [ ] 
- [ ] 
- [ ] 
- [ ] 

## FOLLOW UPS

## APPOINTMENTS

MON

TUE

WED

THU

FRI

SAT

SUN

## SOCIAL MEDIA FOCUS/GOAL THIS WEEK

Just finish the damn thing! Your future self will thank you.

# SOCIAL MEDIA ENGAGEMENT PLAN & TRACKER

ENGAGEMENT ACTIVITY:

| | | SUN | MON | TUE | WED | THU | FRI | SAT |
|---|---|---|---|---|---|---|---|---|
| NOTES: | WK1 | | | | | | | |
| | WK2 | | | | | | | |
| | WK3 | | | | | | | |
| | WK4 | | | | | | | |

ENGAGEMENT ACTIVITY:

| | | SUN | MON | TUE | WED | THU | FRI | SAT |
|---|---|---|---|---|---|---|---|---|
| NOTES: | WK1 | | | | | | | |
| | WK2 | | | | | | | |
| | WK3 | | | | | | | |
| | WK4 | | | | | | | |

ENGAGEMENT ACTIVITY:

| | | SUN | MON | TUE | WED | THU | FRI | SAT |
|---|---|---|---|---|---|---|---|---|
| NOTES: | WK1 | | | | | | | |
| | WK2 | | | | | | | |
| | WK3 | | | | | | | |
| | WK4 | | | | | | | |

ENGAGEMENT ACTIVITY:

| | | SUN | MON | TUE | WED | THU | FRI | SAT |
|---|---|---|---|---|---|---|---|---|
| NOTES: | WK1 | | | | | | | |
| | WK2 | | | | | | | |
| | WK3 | | | | | | | |
| | WK4 | | | | | | | |

ENGAGEMENT ACTIVITY:

| | | SUN | MON | TUE | WED | THU | FRI | SAT |
|---|---|---|---|---|---|---|---|---|
| NOTES: | WK1 | | | | | | | |
| | WK2 | | | | | | | |
| | WK3 | | | | | | | |
| | WK4 | | | | | | | |

# July 2026

27 MONDAY

28 TUESDAY

29 WEDNESDAY

NOTES

30 THURSDAY

31 FRIDAY

1 SATURDAY

2 SUNDAY

National Friendship Day

# July 2026

## MONTH IN REVIEW

I AM GRATEFUL FOR

CONNECTED WITH

PERSONAL WINS

WHAT I LEARNED

GOALS MET

PREFERED PLATFORM GROWTH

TOP PERFORMING POST

Doers — summer flex! What's working? Share your July a-ha in the Plandipity Doer's Inner Circle (Our Private FB Group)

"YOU DON'T HAVE TO BE THE LOUDEST
VOICE IN THE ROOM, JUST
THE ONE THAT *Lifts others up*,
THAT SPEAKS THE TRUTH, AND THAT IS
CLEAR IN YOUR INTENTIONS."

MICHELLE OBAMA

# August 2026

@MORETHANSERENDIPITY

# August 2026

## Business Goal

What's the one thing that will move your business forward this month?

## Personal Goal

What personal win or habit will make life easier or happier?

## Social Media Marketing Planning

### KEY DATES

What holidays, launches, or community events should you post about?

- 
- 
- 
- 
- 

### THIS MONTH'S MARKETING FOCUS

### BUSINESS EVENTS

### PERSONAL EVENTS

**Let's turn your ideas into action!**
**Scan the QR code and plan your August social media content with me.**

# My Tasks This Month

NOTES AND IDEAS

Feeling the mid-year wobble?
Tap the QR to browse what's happening now - free classes, live trainings, and tools designed to make your content feel lighter.

| SUNDAY | MONDAY | TUESDAY | WEDNESDAY |
|---|---|---|---|
| 26 | 27 | 28 | 29 |
| 2 | 3 | 4 | 5 |
| 9 | 10 | 11 | 12 |
| 16 | 17 | 18 | 19 |
| 23 | 24 | 25 | 26 |
| 30 | 31 | 1 | 2 |

# August 2026

| THURSDAY | FRIDAY | SATURDAY |
| --- | --- | --- |
| 30 | 31 | 1 |
| 6 | 7 | 8 |
| 13 | 14 | 15 |
| 20 | 21 | 22<br>CONTENT CABOODLE DROPS TODAY! |
| 27 | 28 | 29 |
| 3 | 4 | 5 |

## Notes

## Reminders

**Doer's: be sure to register for weekly We Plan Wednesdays**

# August 2026

## TOP TO-DOS THIS WEEK

## FOLLOW UPS

## APPOINTMENTS

MON

TUE

WED

THU

FRI

SAT

SUN

## SOCIAL MEDIA FOCUS/GOAL THIS WEEK

Start messy.
*Keep moving*
Get better.

## SOCIAL MEDIA ENGAGEMENT PLAN & TRACKER

ENGAGEMENT ACTIVITY:

| | | SUN | MON | TUE | WED | THU | FRI | SAT |
|---|---|---|---|---|---|---|---|---|
| NOTES: | WK1 | | | | | | | |
| | WK2 | | | | | | | |
| | WK3 | | | | | | | |
| | WK4 | | | | | | | |

ENGAGEMENT ACTIVITY:

| | | SUN | MON | TUE | WED | THU | FRI | SAT |
|---|---|---|---|---|---|---|---|---|
| NOTES: | WK1 | | | | | | | |
| | WK2 | | | | | | | |
| | WK3 | | | | | | | |
| | WK4 | | | | | | | |

ENGAGEMENT ACTIVITY:

| | | SUN | MON | TUE | WED | THU | FRI | SAT |
|---|---|---|---|---|---|---|---|---|
| NOTES: | WK1 | | | | | | | |
| | WK2 | | | | | | | |
| | WK3 | | | | | | | |
| | WK4 | | | | | | | |

ENGAGEMENT ACTIVITY:

| | | SUN | MON | TUE | WED | THU | FRI | SAT |
|---|---|---|---|---|---|---|---|---|
| NOTES: | WK1 | | | | | | | |
| | WK2 | | | | | | | |
| | WK3 | | | | | | | |
| | WK4 | | | | | | | |

ENGAGEMENT ACTIVITY:

| | | SUN | MON | TUE | WED | THU | FRI | SAT |
|---|---|---|---|---|---|---|---|---|
| NOTES: | WK1 | | | | | | | |
| | WK2 | | | | | | | |
| | WK3 | | | | | | | |
| | WK4 | | | | | | | |

# August 2026

3 MONDAY

4 TUESDAY

5 WEDNESDAY

NOTES

6 THURSDAY

7 FRIDAY

8 SATURDAY

9 SUNDAY

National Book Lovers Day

# August 2026

## TOP TO-DOS THIS WEEK

## FOLLOW UPS

## APPOINTMENTS

MON

TUE

WED

THU

FRI

SAT

SUN

## SOCIAL MEDIA FOCUS/GOAL THIS WEEK

Reminder:
Celebrate
what's working.

# SOCIAL MEDIA ENGAGEMENT PLAN & TRACKER

ENGAGEMENT ACTIVITY:

| | | SUN | MON | TUE | WED | THU | FRI | SAT |
|---|---|---|---|---|---|---|---|---|
| NOTES: | WK1 | | | | | | | |
| | WK2 | | | | | | | |
| | WK3 | | | | | | | |
| | WK4 | | | | | | | |

ENGAGEMENT ACTIVITY:

| | | SUN | MON | TUE | WED | THU | FRI | SAT |
|---|---|---|---|---|---|---|---|---|
| NOTES: | WK1 | | | | | | | |
| | WK2 | | | | | | | |
| | WK3 | | | | | | | |
| | WK4 | | | | | | | |

ENGAGEMENT ACTIVITY:

| | | SUN | MON | TUE | WED | THU | FRI | SAT |
|---|---|---|---|---|---|---|---|---|
| NOTES: | WK1 | | | | | | | |
| | WK2 | | | | | | | |
| | WK3 | | | | | | | |
| | WK4 | | | | | | | |

ENGAGEMENT ACTIVITY:

| | | SUN | MON | TUE | WED | THU | FRI | SAT |
|---|---|---|---|---|---|---|---|---|
| NOTES: | WK1 | | | | | | | |
| | WK2 | | | | | | | |
| | WK3 | | | | | | | |
| | WK4 | | | | | | | |

ENGAGEMENT ACTIVITY:

| | | SUN | MON | TUE | WED | THU | FRI | SAT |
|---|---|---|---|---|---|---|---|---|
| NOTES: | WK1 | | | | | | | |
| | WK2 | | | | | | | |
| | WK3 | | | | | | | |
| | WK4 | | | | | | | |

# August 2026

10 MONDAY

11 TUESDAY

12 WEDNESDAY

NOTES

13 THURSDAY

14 FRIDAY

15 SATURDAY

16 SUNDAY

# August 2026

## TOP TO-DOS THIS WEEK

- [ ] 
- [ ] 
- [ ] 
- [ ] 
- [ ] 
- [ ] 

## FOLLOW UPS

## APPOINTMENTS

MON

TUE

WED

THU

FRI

SAT

SUN

## SOCIAL MEDIA FOCUS/GOAL THIS WEEK

Perfect is boring.

*Progress* is brave!

# SOCIAL MEDIA ENGAGEMENT PLAN & TRACKER

ENGAGEMENT ACTIVITY:

| | | SUN | MON | TUE | WED | THU | FRI | SAT |
|---|---|---|---|---|---|---|---|---|
| NOTES: | WK1 | | | | | | | |
| | WK2 | | | | | | | |
| | WK3 | | | | | | | |
| | WK4 | | | | | | | |

ENGAGEMENT ACTIVITY:

| | | SUN | MON | TUE | WED | THU | FRI | SAT |
|---|---|---|---|---|---|---|---|---|
| NOTES: | WK1 | | | | | | | |
| | WK2 | | | | | | | |
| | WK3 | | | | | | | |
| | WK4 | | | | | | | |

ENGAGEMENT ACTIVITY:

| | | SUN | MON | TUE | WED | THU | FRI | SAT |
|---|---|---|---|---|---|---|---|---|
| NOTES: | WK1 | | | | | | | |
| | WK2 | | | | | | | |
| | WK3 | | | | | | | |
| | WK4 | | | | | | | |

ENGAGEMENT ACTIVITY:

| | | SUN | MON | TUE | WED | THU | FRI | SAT |
|---|---|---|---|---|---|---|---|---|
| NOTES: | WK1 | | | | | | | |
| | WK2 | | | | | | | |
| | WK3 | | | | | | | |
| | WK4 | | | | | | | |

ENGAGEMENT ACTIVITY:

| | | SUN | MON | TUE | WED | THU | FRI | SAT |
|---|---|---|---|---|---|---|---|---|
| NOTES: | WK1 | | | | | | | |
| | WK2 | | | | | | | |
| | WK3 | | | | | | | |
| | WK4 | | | | | | | |

# August 2026

17 MONDAY

18 TUESDAY

19 WEDNESDAY

NOTES

20 THURSDAY

21 FRIDAY

22 SATURDAY

23 SUNDAY

# August 2026

## TOP TO-DOS THIS WEEK

- [ ] 
- [ ] 
- [ ] 
- [ ] 
- [ ] 
- [ ] 

## FOLLOW UPS

## APPOINTMENTS

MON

TUE

WED

THU

FRI

SAT

SUN

## SOCIAL MEDIA FOCUS/GOAL THIS WEEK

Permission granted: become wildly you!

# SOCIAL MEDIA ENGAGEMENT PLAN & TRACKER

ENGAGEMENT ACTIVITY:

| | | SUN | MON | TUE | WED | THU | FRI | SAT |
|---|---|---|---|---|---|---|---|---|
| NOTES: | WK1 | | | | | | | |
| | WK2 | | | | | | | |
| | WK3 | | | | | | | |
| | WK4 | | | | | | | |

ENGAGEMENT ACTIVITY:

| | | SUN | MON | TUE | WED | THU | FRI | SAT |
|---|---|---|---|---|---|---|---|---|
| NOTES: | WK1 | | | | | | | |
| | WK2 | | | | | | | |
| | WK3 | | | | | | | |
| | WK4 | | | | | | | |

ENGAGEMENT ACTIVITY:

| | | SUN | MON | TUE | WED | THU | FRI | SAT |
|---|---|---|---|---|---|---|---|---|
| NOTES: | WK1 | | | | | | | |
| | WK2 | | | | | | | |
| | WK3 | | | | | | | |
| | WK4 | | | | | | | |

ENGAGEMENT ACTIVITY:

| | | SUN | MON | TUE | WED | THU | FRI | SAT |
|---|---|---|---|---|---|---|---|---|
| NOTES: | WK1 | | | | | | | |
| | WK2 | | | | | | | |
| | WK3 | | | | | | | |
| | WK4 | | | | | | | |

ENGAGEMENT ACTIVITY:

| | | SUN | MON | TUE | WED | THU | FRI | SAT |
|---|---|---|---|---|---|---|---|---|
| NOTES: | WK1 | | | | | | | |
| | WK2 | | | | | | | |
| | WK3 | | | | | | | |
| | WK4 | | | | | | | |

# August 2026

24 MONDAY

25 TUESDAY

26 WEDNESDAY

NOTES

27 THURSDAY

28 FRIDAY

National Thoughtful Day

29 SATURDAY

30 SUNDAY

# August 2026

## MONTH IN REVIEW

I AM GRATEFUL FOR

CONNECTED WITH

PERSONAL WINS

WHAT I LEARNED

GOALS MET

PREFERED PLATFORM GROWTH

TOP PERFORMING POST

**Doers — audit + adjust: tell us one August lesson you're taking forward in the Plandipity Doer's Inner Circle (Our Private FB Group)**

"THE QUESTION ISN'T WHO'S GOING TO LET ME; IT'S WHO'S GOING TO *Stop me.*"

AYN RAND

# *September* 2026

# September 2026

## Business Goal

What's the one thing that will move your business forward this month?

## Personal Goal

What personal win or habit will make life easier or happier?

## Social Media Marketing Planning

### KEY DATES

What holidays, launches, or community events should you post about?

- ____________________
- ____________________
- ____________________
- ____________________
- ____________________

### THIS MONTH'S MARKETING FOCUS

### BUSINESS EVENTS

### PERSONAL EVENTS

PLAN WITH ME!

**New season, new momentum!**
**Scan the QR code to plan your September content and finish strong!**

# My Tasks This Month

## NOTES AND IDEAS

# September 2026

| SUNDAY | MONDAY | TUESDAY | WEDNESDAY |
|---|---|---|---|
| 30 | 31 | 1 | 2 |
| 6 | 7 | 8 | 9 |
| 13 | 14 | 15 | 16 |
| 20 | 21 | 22 | 23 |
| 27 | 28 | 29 | 30 |

| THURSDAY | FRIDAY | SATURDAY |
| --- | --- | --- |
| 3 | 4 | 5 |
| 10 | 11 | 12 |
| 17 | 18 | 19<br>CONTENT<br>CABOODLE<br>DROPS TODAY! |
| 24 | 25 | 26 |
| 1 | 2 | 3 |

## Notes

## Reminders

**Doer's: be sure to register for weekly We Plan Wednesdays**

# September 2026

## TOP TO-DOS THIS WEEK

- [ ] 
- [ ] 
- [ ] 
- [ ] 
- [ ] 
- [ ] 

## FOLLOW UPS

## APPOINTMENTS

MON

TUE

WED

THU

FRI

SAT

SUN

## SOCIAL MEDIA FOCUS/GOAL THIS WEEK

Boundaries are a form of self-respect.

## SOCIAL MEDIA ENGAGEMENT PLAN & TRACKER

ENGAGEMENT ACTIVITY:

| | | SUN | MON | TUE | WED | THU | FRI | SAT |
|---|---|---|---|---|---|---|---|---|
| NOTES: | WK1 | | | | | | | |
| | WK2 | | | | | | | |
| | WK3 | | | | | | | |
| | WK4 | | | | | | | |

ENGAGEMENT ACTIVITY:

| | | SUN | MON | TUE | WED | THU | FRI | SAT |
|---|---|---|---|---|---|---|---|---|
| NOTES: | WK1 | | | | | | | |
| | WK2 | | | | | | | |
| | WK3 | | | | | | | |
| | WK4 | | | | | | | |

ENGAGEMENT ACTIVITY:

| | | SUN | MON | TUE | WED | THU | FRI | SAT |
|---|---|---|---|---|---|---|---|---|
| NOTES: | WK1 | | | | | | | |
| | WK2 | | | | | | | |
| | WK3 | | | | | | | |
| | WK4 | | | | | | | |

ENGAGEMENT ACTIVITY:

| | | SUN | MON | TUE | WED | THU | FRI | SAT |
|---|---|---|---|---|---|---|---|---|
| NOTES: | WK1 | | | | | | | |
| | WK2 | | | | | | | |
| | WK3 | | | | | | | |
| | WK4 | | | | | | | |

ENGAGEMENT ACTIVITY:

| | | SUN | MON | TUE | WED | THU | FRI | SAT |
|---|---|---|---|---|---|---|---|---|
| NOTES: | WK1 | | | | | | | |
| | WK2 | | | | | | | |
| | WK3 | | | | | | | |
| | WK4 | | | | | | | |

# September 2026

31 MONDAY

1 TUESDAY

2 WEDNESDAY

NOTES

3 THURSDAY

4 FRIDAY

5 SATURDAY

6 SUNDAY

# September 2026

## TOP TO-DOS THIS WEEK

- [ ] 
- [ ] 
- [ ] 
- [ ] 
- [ ] 
- [ ] 

## FOLLOW UPS

## APPOINTMENTS

MON

TUE

WED

THU

FRI

SAT

SUN

## SOCIAL MEDIA FOCUS/GOAL THIS WEEK

You're not behind,
you're building
*momentum!*

# SOCIAL MEDIA ENGAGEMENT PLAN & TRACKER

ENGAGEMENT ACTIVITY:

| | | SUN | MON | TUE | WED | THU | FRI | SAT |
|---|---|---|---|---|---|---|---|---|
| NOTES: | WK1 | | | | | | | |
| | WK2 | | | | | | | |
| | WK3 | | | | | | | |
| | WK4 | | | | | | | |

ENGAGEMENT ACTIVITY:

| | | SUN | MON | TUE | WED | THU | FRI | SAT |
|---|---|---|---|---|---|---|---|---|
| NOTES: | WK1 | | | | | | | |
| | WK2 | | | | | | | |
| | WK3 | | | | | | | |
| | WK4 | | | | | | | |

ENGAGEMENT ACTIVITY:

| | | SUN | MON | TUE | WED | THU | FRI | SAT |
|---|---|---|---|---|---|---|---|---|
| NOTES: | WK1 | | | | | | | |
| | WK2 | | | | | | | |
| | WK3 | | | | | | | |
| | WK4 | | | | | | | |

ENGAGEMENT ACTIVITY:

| | | SUN | MON | TUE | WED | THU | FRI | SAT |
|---|---|---|---|---|---|---|---|---|
| NOTES: | WK1 | | | | | | | |
| | WK2 | | | | | | | |
| | WK3 | | | | | | | |
| | WK4 | | | | | | | |

ENGAGEMENT ACTIVITY:

| | | SUN | MON | TUE | WED | THU | FRI | SAT |
|---|---|---|---|---|---|---|---|---|
| NOTES: | WK1 | | | | | | | |
| | WK2 | | | | | | | |
| | WK3 | | | | | | | |
| | WK4 | | | | | | | |

# September 2026

7 MONDAY Labor Day

8 TUESDAY

9 WEDNESDAY

NOTES

10 THURSDAY

National Plandipity Doer's Day

Applied For!

11 FRIDAY

Patriot Day

12 SATURDAY

National Day of Encouragement

13 SUNDAY

# September 2026

## TOP TO-DOS THIS WEEK

- [ ] 
- [ ] 
- [ ] 
- [ ] 
- [ ] 
- [ ] 

## FOLLOW UPS

## APPOINTMENTS

MON

TUE

WED

THU

FRI

SAT

SUN

## SOCIAL MEDIA FOCUS/GOAL THIS WEEK

Stay grounded in who you are, and rise into who you're becoming.

# SOCIAL MEDIA ENGAGEMENT PLAN & TRACKER

ENGAGEMENT ACTIVITY:

| | | SUN | MON | TUE | WED | THU | FRI | SAT |
|---|---|---|---|---|---|---|---|---|
| NOTES: | WK1 | | | | | | | |
| | WK2 | | | | | | | |
| | WK3 | | | | | | | |
| | WK4 | | | | | | | |

ENGAGEMENT ACTIVITY:

| | | SUN | MON | TUE | WED | THU | FRI | SAT |
|---|---|---|---|---|---|---|---|---|
| NOTES: | WK1 | | | | | | | |
| | WK2 | | | | | | | |
| | WK3 | | | | | | | |
| | WK4 | | | | | | | |

ENGAGEMENT ACTIVITY:

| | | SUN | MON | TUE | WED | THU | FRI | SAT |
|---|---|---|---|---|---|---|---|---|
| NOTES: | WK1 | | | | | | | |
| | WK2 | | | | | | | |
| | WK3 | | | | | | | |
| | WK4 | | | | | | | |

ENGAGEMENT ACTIVITY:

| | | SUN | MON | TUE | WED | THU | FRI | SAT |
|---|---|---|---|---|---|---|---|---|
| NOTES: | WK1 | | | | | | | |
| | WK2 | | | | | | | |
| | WK3 | | | | | | | |
| | WK4 | | | | | | | |

ENGAGEMENT ACTIVITY:

| | | SUN | MON | TUE | WED | THU | FRI | SAT |
|---|---|---|---|---|---|---|---|---|
| NOTES: | WK1 | | | | | | | |
| | WK2 | | | | | | | |
| | WK3 | | | | | | | |
| | WK4 | | | | | | | |

# September 2026

14 MONDAY

15 TUESDAY

16 WEDNESDAY

NOTES

17 THURSDAY

18 FRIDAY

19 SATURDAY

20 SUNDAY

# September 2026

## TOP TO-DOS THIS WEEK

## FOLLOW UPS

## APPOINTMENTS

MON

TUE

WED

THU

FRI

SAT

SUN

## SOCIAL MEDIA FOCUS/GOAL THIS WEEK

Empty doesn't serve anyone. Refill unapologetically.

# SOCIAL MEDIA ENGAGEMENT PLAN & TRACKER

ENGAGEMENT ACTIVITY:

| | | SUN | MON | TUE | WED | THU | FRI | SAT |
|---|---|---|---|---|---|---|---|---|
| NOTES: | WK1 | | | | | | | |
| | WK2 | | | | | | | |
| | WK3 | | | | | | | |
| | WK4 | | | | | | | |

ENGAGEMENT ACTIVITY:

| | | SUN | MON | TUE | WED | THU | FRI | SAT |
|---|---|---|---|---|---|---|---|---|
| NOTES: | WK1 | | | | | | | |
| | WK2 | | | | | | | |
| | WK3 | | | | | | | |
| | WK4 | | | | | | | |

ENGAGEMENT ACTIVITY:

| | | SUN | MON | TUE | WED | THU | FRI | SAT |
|---|---|---|---|---|---|---|---|---|
| NOTES: | WK1 | | | | | | | |
| | WK2 | | | | | | | |
| | WK3 | | | | | | | |
| | WK4 | | | | | | | |

ENGAGEMENT ACTIVITY:

| | | SUN | MON | TUE | WED | THU | FRI | SAT |
|---|---|---|---|---|---|---|---|---|
| NOTES: | WK1 | | | | | | | |
| | WK2 | | | | | | | |
| | WK3 | | | | | | | |
| | WK4 | | | | | | | |

ENGAGEMENT ACTIVITY:

| | | SUN | MON | TUE | WED | THU | FRI | SAT |
|---|---|---|---|---|---|---|---|---|
| NOTES: | WK1 | | | | | | | |
| | WK2 | | | | | | | |
| | WK3 | | | | | | | |
| | WK4 | | | | | | | |

# September 2026

21 MONDAY

22 TUESDAY

First Day Of Fall

American Business Women's Day

23 WEDNESDAY

NOTES

24 THURSDAY

25 FRIDAY

26 SATURDAY

27 SUNDAY

# September 2026

## TOP TO-DOS THIS WEEK

## FOLLOW UPS

## APPOINTMENTS

MON

TUE

WED

THU

FRI

SAT

SUN

## SOCIAL MEDIA FOCUS/GOAL THIS WEEK

Take action,
even if it's small
- you got this!

# SOCIAL MEDIA ENGAGEMENT PLAN & TRACKER

ENGAGEMENT ACTIVITY:

| | | SUN | MON | TUE | WED | THU | FRI | SAT |
|---|---|---|---|---|---|---|---|---|
| NOTES: | WK1 | | | | | | | |
| | WK2 | | | | | | | |
| | WK3 | | | | | | | |
| | WK4 | | | | | | | |

ENGAGEMENT ACTIVITY:

| | | SUN | MON | TUE | WED | THU | FRI | SAT |
|---|---|---|---|---|---|---|---|---|
| NOTES: | WK1 | | | | | | | |
| | WK2 | | | | | | | |
| | WK3 | | | | | | | |
| | WK4 | | | | | | | |

ENGAGEMENT ACTIVITY:

| | | SUN | MON | TUE | WED | THU | FRI | SAT |
|---|---|---|---|---|---|---|---|---|
| NOTES: | WK1 | | | | | | | |
| | WK2 | | | | | | | |
| | WK3 | | | | | | | |
| | WK4 | | | | | | | |

ENGAGEMENT ACTIVITY:

| | | SUN | MON | TUE | WED | THU | FRI | SAT |
|---|---|---|---|---|---|---|---|---|
| NOTES: | WK1 | | | | | | | |
| | WK2 | | | | | | | |
| | WK3 | | | | | | | |
| | WK4 | | | | | | | |

ENGAGEMENT ACTIVITY:

| | | SUN | MON | TUE | WED | THU | FRI | SAT |
|---|---|---|---|---|---|---|---|---|
| NOTES: | WK1 | | | | | | | |
| | WK2 | | | | | | | |
| | WK3 | | | | | | | |
| | WK4 | | | | | | | |

# September 2026

28 MONDAY

29 TUESDAY

30 WEDNESDAY

NOTES

1 THURSDAY

2 FRIDAY

3 SATURDAY

4 SUNDAY

# September 2026

## MONTH IN REVIEW

I AM GRATEFUL FOR

CONNECTED WITH

PERSONAL WINS

WHAT I LEARNED

GOALS MET

PREFERED PLATFORM GROWTH

TOP PERFORMING POST

**Doers — fresh start energy: drop your September breakthrough in the Plandipity Doer's Inner Circle (Our Private FB Group.)**

"YOU CAN BE A MASTERPIECE AND *a work in progress* AT THE SAME TIME."

SOPHIA BUSH

# October 2026

# October 2026

## Business Goal

What's the one thing that will move your business forward this month?

## Personal Goal

What personal win or habit will make life easier or happier?

## Social Media Marketing Planning

### KEY DATES

What holidays, launches, or community events should you post about?

- ☐ ______________________
- ☐ ______________________
- ☐ ______________________
- ☐ ______________________
- ☐ ______________________

### THIS MONTH'S MARKETING FOCUS

### BUSINESS EVENTS

### PERSONAL EVENTS

PLAN WITH ME!

**Let's get creative and a little spooky.**
**Scan the QR code and plan your October content with me.**

# My Tasks This Month

## NOTES AND IDEAS

# October 2026

| SUNDAY | MONDAY | TUESDAY | WEDNESDAY |
|---|---|---|---|
| 27 | 28 | 29 | 30 |
| 4 | 5 | 6 | 7 |
| 11 | 12 | 13 | 14 |
| 18 | 19 | 20 | 21 |
| 25 | 26 | 27 | 28 |

| THURSDAY | FRIDAY | SATURDAY |
| --- | --- | --- |
| 1 | 2 | 3 |
| 8 | 9 | 10 |
| 15 | 16 | 17<br>CONTENT CABOODLE DROPS TODAY! |
| 22 | 23 | 24 |
| 29 | 30 | 31 |

Notes

Reminders

Doer's: be sure to register for weekly We Plan Wednesdays

# October 2026

## TOP TO-DOS THIS WEEK

- [ ] 
- [ ] 
- [ ] 
- [ ] 
- [ ] 
- [ ] 

## FOLLOW UPS

## APPOINTMENTS

MON

TUE

WED

THU

FRI

SAT

SUN

## SOCIAL MEDIA FOCUS/GOAL THIS WEEK

Embrace the plot twist - you wrote the story, remember?

## SOCIAL MEDIA ENGAGEMENT PLAN & TRACKER

ENGAGEMENT ACTIVITY:

| | | SUN | MON | TUE | WED | THU | FRI | SAT |
|---|---|---|---|---|---|---|---|---|
| NOTES: | WK1 | | | | | | | |
| | WK2 | | | | | | | |
| | WK3 | | | | | | | |
| | WK4 | | | | | | | |

ENGAGEMENT ACTIVITY:

| | | SUN | MON | TUE | WED | THU | FRI | SAT |
|---|---|---|---|---|---|---|---|---|
| NOTES: | WK1 | | | | | | | |
| | WK2 | | | | | | | |
| | WK3 | | | | | | | |
| | WK4 | | | | | | | |

ENGAGEMENT ACTIVITY:

| | | SUN | MON | TUE | WED | THU | FRI | SAT |
|---|---|---|---|---|---|---|---|---|
| NOTES: | WK1 | | | | | | | |
| | WK2 | | | | | | | |
| | WK3 | | | | | | | |
| | WK4 | | | | | | | |

ENGAGEMENT ACTIVITY:

| | | SUN | MON | TUE | WED | THU | FRI | SAT |
|---|---|---|---|---|---|---|---|---|
| NOTES: | WK1 | | | | | | | |
| | WK2 | | | | | | | |
| | WK3 | | | | | | | |
| | WK4 | | | | | | | |

ENGAGEMENT ACTIVITY:

| | | SUN | MON | TUE | WED | THU | FRI | SAT |
|---|---|---|---|---|---|---|---|---|
| NOTES: | WK1 | | | | | | | |
| | WK2 | | | | | | | |
| | WK3 | | | | | | | |
| | WK4 | | | | | | | |

# October 2026

5 MONDAY

6 TUESDAY

7 WEDNESDAY

NOTES

8 THURSDAY

9 FRIDAY

10 SATURDAY

11 SUNDAY

# October 2026

## TOP TO-DOS THIS WEEK

- [ ] 
- [ ] 
- [ ] 
- [ ] 
- [ ] 
- [ ] 

## FOLLOW UPS

## APPOINTMENTS

MON

TUE

WED

THU

FRI

SAT

SUN

## SOCIAL MEDIA FOCUS/GOAL THIS WEEK

The voice that doubts you doesn't know your power.

# SOCIAL MEDIA ENGAGEMENT PLAN & TRACKER

ENGAGEMENT ACTIVITY:

| | | SUN | MON | TUE | WED | THU | FRI | SAT |
|---|---|---|---|---|---|---|---|---|
| NOTES: | WK1 | | | | | | | |
| | WK2 | | | | | | | |
| | WK3 | | | | | | | |
| | WK4 | | | | | | | |

ENGAGEMENT ACTIVITY:

| | | SUN | MON | TUE | WED | THU | FRI | SAT |
|---|---|---|---|---|---|---|---|---|
| NOTES: | WK1 | | | | | | | |
| | WK2 | | | | | | | |
| | WK3 | | | | | | | |
| | WK4 | | | | | | | |

ENGAGEMENT ACTIVITY:

| | | SUN | MON | TUE | WED | THU | FRI | SAT |
|---|---|---|---|---|---|---|---|---|
| NOTES: | WK1 | | | | | | | |
| | WK2 | | | | | | | |
| | WK3 | | | | | | | |
| | WK4 | | | | | | | |

ENGAGEMENT ACTIVITY:

| | | SUN | MON | TUE | WED | THU | FRI | SAT |
|---|---|---|---|---|---|---|---|---|
| NOTES: | WK1 | | | | | | | |
| | WK2 | | | | | | | |
| | WK3 | | | | | | | |
| | WK4 | | | | | | | |

ENGAGEMENT ACTIVITY:

| | | SUN | MON | TUE | WED | THU | FRI | SAT |
|---|---|---|---|---|---|---|---|---|
| NOTES: | WK1 | | | | | | | |
| | WK2 | | | | | | | |
| | WK3 | | | | | | | |
| | WK4 | | | | | | | |

# October 2026

12 MONDAY

13 TUESDAY

14 WEDNESDAY

NOTES

15 THURSDAY

16 FRIDAY

Boss's Day

17 SATURDAY

18 SUNDAY

# October 2026

## TOP TO-DOS THIS WEEK

- 
- 
- 
- 
- 
- 

## FOLLOW UPS

## APPOINTMENTS

MON

TUE

WED

THU

FRI

SAT

SUN

## SOCIAL MEDIA FOCUS/GOAL THIS WEEK

Give yourself *grace*, then keep going.

# SOCIAL MEDIA ENGAGEMENT PLAN & TRACKER

ENGAGEMENT ACTIVITY:

| | | SUN | MON | TUE | WED | THU | FRI | SAT |
|---|---|---|---|---|---|---|---|---|
| NOTES: | WK1 | | | | | | | |
| | WK2 | | | | | | | |
| | WK3 | | | | | | | |
| | WK4 | | | | | | | |

ENGAGEMENT ACTIVITY:

| | | SUN | MON | TUE | WED | THU | FRI | SAT |
|---|---|---|---|---|---|---|---|---|
| NOTES: | WK1 | | | | | | | |
| | WK2 | | | | | | | |
| | WK3 | | | | | | | |
| | WK4 | | | | | | | |

ENGAGEMENT ACTIVITY:

| | | SUN | MON | TUE | WED | THU | FRI | SAT |
|---|---|---|---|---|---|---|---|---|
| NOTES: | WK1 | | | | | | | |
| | WK2 | | | | | | | |
| | WK3 | | | | | | | |
| | WK4 | | | | | | | |

ENGAGEMENT ACTIVITY:

| | | SUN | MON | TUE | WED | THU | FRI | SAT |
|---|---|---|---|---|---|---|---|---|
| NOTES: | WK1 | | | | | | | |
| | WK2 | | | | | | | |
| | WK3 | | | | | | | |
| | WK4 | | | | | | | |

ENGAGEMENT ACTIVITY:

| | | SUN | MON | TUE | WED | THU | FRI | SAT |
|---|---|---|---|---|---|---|---|---|
| NOTES: | WK1 | | | | | | | |
| | WK2 | | | | | | | |
| | WK3 | | | | | | | |
| | WK4 | | | | | | | |

# October 2026

19 MONDAY

20 TUESDAY

21 WEDNESDAY Support Your Local Chamber of Commerce Day

NOTES

22 THURSDAY

23 FRIDAY

24 SATURDAY

National Make A Difference Day

25 SUNDAY

# October 2026

## TOP TO-DOS THIS WEEK

- [ ] 
- [ ] 
- [ ] 
- [ ] 
- [ ] 
- [ ] 

## FOLLOW UPS

## APPOINTMENTS

MON

TUE

WED

THU

FRI

SAT

SUN

## SOCIAL MEDIA FOCUS/GOAL THIS WEEK

Change is uncomfortable, so is staying stuck.

# SOCIAL MEDIA ENGAGEMENT PLAN & TRACKER

ENGAGEMENT ACTIVITY:

| | | SUN | MON | TUE | WED | THU | FRI | SAT |
|---|---|---|---|---|---|---|---|---|
| NOTES: | WK1 | | | | | | | |
| | WK2 | | | | | | | |
| | WK3 | | | | | | | |
| | WK4 | | | | | | | |

ENGAGEMENT ACTIVITY:

| | | SUN | MON | TUE | WED | THU | FRI | SAT |
|---|---|---|---|---|---|---|---|---|
| NOTES: | WK1 | | | | | | | |
| | WK2 | | | | | | | |
| | WK3 | | | | | | | |
| | WK4 | | | | | | | |

ENGAGEMENT ACTIVITY:

| | | SUN | MON | TUE | WED | THU | FRI | SAT |
|---|---|---|---|---|---|---|---|---|
| NOTES: | WK1 | | | | | | | |
| | WK2 | | | | | | | |
| | WK3 | | | | | | | |
| | WK4 | | | | | | | |

ENGAGEMENT ACTIVITY:

| | | SUN | MON | TUE | WED | THU | FRI | SAT |
|---|---|---|---|---|---|---|---|---|
| NOTES: | WK1 | | | | | | | |
| | WK2 | | | | | | | |
| | WK3 | | | | | | | |
| | WK4 | | | | | | | |

ENGAGEMENT ACTIVITY:

| | | SUN | MON | TUE | WED | THU | FRI | SAT |
|---|---|---|---|---|---|---|---|---|
| NOTES: | WK1 | | | | | | | |
| | WK2 | | | | | | | |
| | WK3 | | | | | | | |
| | WK4 | | | | | | | |

# October 2026

26 MONDAY

27 TUESDAY

28 WEDNESDAY

NOTES

29 THURSDAY

30 FRIDAY

31 SATURDAY

Happy Halloween

1 SUNDAY

Daylight Saving Time Ends

# October 2026

## MONTH IN REVIEW

I AM GRATEFUL FOR

CONNECTED WITH

PERSONAL WINS

WHAT I LEARNED

GOALS MET

PREFERED PLATFORM GROWTH

TOP PERFORMING POST

Doers — spooky good progress? Share your October a-ha in the Plandipity Doer's Inner Circle (Our Private FB Group).

"DON'T EVER DOUBT YOUR WORTH OR
*the impact you're making.*
SUCCESS IS PERSONAL
— DEFINE IT YOUR WAY."

**BEYONCÉ**

# November 2026

# November 2026

## Business Goal

What's the one thing that will move your business forward this month?

## Personal Goal

What personal win or habit will make life easier or happier?

## Social Media Marketing Planning

### KEY DATES

What holidays, launches, or community events should you post about?

### THIS MONTH'S MARKETING FOCUS

### BUSINESS EVENTS

### PERSONAL EVENTS

**Gratitude + growth = great content.**
**Scan the QR code to plan your November social media strategy!**

# My Tasks This Month

NOTES AND IDEAS

This is the season for simplicity. Scan here to see all available trainings—free, paid, live, and downloadable, so you can get exactly what you need, when you need it.

# November 2026

| SUNDAY | MONDAY | TUESDAY | WEDNESDAY |
|---|---|---|---|
| 1 | 2 | 3 | 4 |
| 8 | 9 | 10 | 11 |
| 15 | 16 | 17 | 18 |
| 22 | 23 | 24 | 25 |
| 29 | 30 | 1 | 2 |

| THURSDAY | FRIDAY | SATURDAY |
| --- | --- | --- |
| 5 | 6 | 7 |
| 12 | 13 | 14 |
| 19 | 20 | 21<br>CONTENT CABOODLE DROPS TODAY! |
| 26 | 27 | 28 |
| 3 | 4 | 5 |

## Notes

## Reminders

**Doer's: be sure to register for weekly We Plan Wednesdays**

# November 2026

## TOP TO-DOS THIS WEEK

- [ ] 
- [ ] 
- [ ] 
- [ ] 
- [ ] 
- [ ] 

## FOLLOW UPS

## APPOINTMENTS

MON

TUE

WED

THU

FRI

SAT

SUN

## SOCIAL MEDIA FOCUS/GOAL THIS WEEK

Gratitude changes your perspective.

## SOCIAL MEDIA ENGAGEMENT PLAN & TRACKER

ENGAGEMENT ACTIVITY:

| | | SUN | MON | TUE | WED | THU | FRI | SAT |
|---|---|---|---|---|---|---|---|---|
| NOTES: | WK1 | | | | | | | |
| | WK2 | | | | | | | |
| | WK3 | | | | | | | |
| | WK4 | | | | | | | |

ENGAGEMENT ACTIVITY:

| | | SUN | MON | TUE | WED | THU | FRI | SAT |
|---|---|---|---|---|---|---|---|---|
| NOTES: | WK1 | | | | | | | |
| | WK2 | | | | | | | |
| | WK3 | | | | | | | |
| | WK4 | | | | | | | |

ENGAGEMENT ACTIVITY:

| | | SUN | MON | TUE | WED | THU | FRI | SAT |
|---|---|---|---|---|---|---|---|---|
| NOTES: | WK1 | | | | | | | |
| | WK2 | | | | | | | |
| | WK3 | | | | | | | |
| | WK4 | | | | | | | |

ENGAGEMENT ACTIVITY:

| | | SUN | MON | TUE | WED | THU | FRI | SAT |
|---|---|---|---|---|---|---|---|---|
| NOTES: | WK1 | | | | | | | |
| | WK2 | | | | | | | |
| | WK3 | | | | | | | |
| | WK4 | | | | | | | |

ENGAGEMENT ACTIVITY:

| | | SUN | MON | TUE | WED | THU | FRI | SAT |
|---|---|---|---|---|---|---|---|---|
| NOTES: | WK1 | | | | | | | |
| | WK2 | | | | | | | |
| | WK3 | | | | | | | |
| | WK4 | | | | | | | |

# November 2026

2 MONDAY

3 TUESDAY

Election Day

4 WEDNESDAY

National Stress Awareness Day

NOTES

5 THURSDAY

6 FRIDAY

76 SATURDAY

8 SUNDAY

# November 2026

## TOP TO-DOS THIS WEEK

- [ ] 
- [ ] 
- [ ] 
- [ ] 
- [ ] 
- [ ] 

## FOLLOW UPS

## APPOINTMENTS

MON

TUE

WED

THU

FRI

SAT

SUN

## SOCIAL MEDIA FOCUS/GOAL THIS WEEK

Your light
inspires others.
Don't dim it to fit in.

## SOCIAL MEDIA ENGAGEMENT PLAN & TRACKER

ENGAGEMENT ACTIVITY:

| | | SUN | MON | TUE | WED | THU | FRI | SAT |
|---|---|---|---|---|---|---|---|---|
| NOTES: | WK1 | | | | | | | |
| | WK2 | | | | | | | |
| | WK3 | | | | | | | |
| | WK4 | | | | | | | |

ENGAGEMENT ACTIVITY:

| | | SUN | MON | TUE | WED | THU | FRI | SAT |
|---|---|---|---|---|---|---|---|---|
| NOTES: | WK1 | | | | | | | |
| | WK2 | | | | | | | |
| | WK3 | | | | | | | |
| | WK4 | | | | | | | |

ENGAGEMENT ACTIVITY:

| | | SUN | MON | TUE | WED | THU | FRI | SAT |
|---|---|---|---|---|---|---|---|---|
| NOTES: | WK1 | | | | | | | |
| | WK2 | | | | | | | |
| | WK3 | | | | | | | |
| | WK4 | | | | | | | |

ENGAGEMENT ACTIVITY:

| | | SUN | MON | TUE | WED | THU | FRI | SAT |
|---|---|---|---|---|---|---|---|---|
| NOTES: | WK1 | | | | | | | |
| | WK2 | | | | | | | |
| | WK3 | | | | | | | |
| | WK4 | | | | | | | |

ENGAGEMENT ACTIVITY:

| | | SUN | MON | TUE | WED | THU | FRI | SAT |
|---|---|---|---|---|---|---|---|---|
| NOTES: | WK1 | | | | | | | |
| | WK2 | | | | | | | |
| | WK3 | | | | | | | |
| | WK4 | | | | | | | |

# November 2026

9 MONDAY

10 TUESDAY

11 WEDNESDAY

Veterans Day

NOTES

12 THURSDAY

13 FRIDAY

14 SATURDAY

15 SUNDAY

# November 2026

## TOP TO-DOS THIS WEEK

## FOLLOW UPS

## APPOINTMENTS

MON

TUE

WED

THU

FRI

SAT

SUN

## SOCIAL MEDIA FOCUS/GOAL THIS WEEK

Ground yourself in *gratitude.* Then go shake things up.

## SOCIAL MEDIA ENGAGEMENT PLAN & TRACKER

ENGAGEMENT ACTIVITY:

| | | SUN | MON | TUE | WED | THU | FRI | SAT |
|---|---|---|---|---|---|---|---|---|
| NOTES: | WK1 | | | | | | | |
| | WK2 | | | | | | | |
| | WK3 | | | | | | | |
| | WK4 | | | | | | | |

ENGAGEMENT ACTIVITY:

| | | SUN | MON | TUE | WED | THU | FRI | SAT |
|---|---|---|---|---|---|---|---|---|
| NOTES: | WK1 | | | | | | | |
| | WK2 | | | | | | | |
| | WK3 | | | | | | | |
| | WK4 | | | | | | | |

ENGAGEMENT ACTIVITY:

| | | SUN | MON | TUE | WED | THU | FRI | SAT |
|---|---|---|---|---|---|---|---|---|
| NOTES: | WK1 | | | | | | | |
| | WK2 | | | | | | | |
| | WK3 | | | | | | | |
| | WK4 | | | | | | | |

ENGAGEMENT ACTIVITY:

| | | SUN | MON | TUE | WED | THU | FRI | SAT |
|---|---|---|---|---|---|---|---|---|
| NOTES: | WK1 | | | | | | | |
| | WK2 | | | | | | | |
| | WK3 | | | | | | | |
| | WK4 | | | | | | | |

ENGAGEMENT ACTIVITY:

| | | SUN | MON | TUE | WED | THU | FRI | SAT |
|---|---|---|---|---|---|---|---|---|
| NOTES: | WK1 | | | | | | | |
| | WK2 | | | | | | | |
| | WK3 | | | | | | | |
| | WK4 | | | | | | | |

# November 2026

16 MONDAY

17 TUESDAY

18 WEDNESDAY

NOTES

19 THURSDAY

20 FRIDAY

21 SATURDAY

22 SUNDAY

# November 2026

## TOP TO-DOS THIS WEEK

- [ ] 
- [ ] 
- [ ] 
- [ ] 
- [ ] 
- [ ] 

## FOLLOW UPS

## APPOINTMENTS

MON

TUE

WED

THU

FRI

SAT

SUN

## SOCIAL MEDIA FOCUS/GOAL THIS WEEK

Rest like it's on your to-do list because it damn well is!

# SOCIAL MEDIA ENGAGEMENT PLAN & TRACKER

ENGAGEMENT ACTIVITY:

| | | SUN | MON | TUE | WED | THU | FRI | SAT |
|---|---|---|---|---|---|---|---|---|
| NOTES: | WK1 | | | | | | | |
| | WK2 | | | | | | | |
| | WK3 | | | | | | | |
| | WK4 | | | | | | | |

ENGAGEMENT ACTIVITY:

| | | SUN | MON | TUE | WED | THU | FRI | SAT |
|---|---|---|---|---|---|---|---|---|
| NOTES: | WK1 | | | | | | | |
| | WK2 | | | | | | | |
| | WK3 | | | | | | | |
| | WK4 | | | | | | | |

ENGAGEMENT ACTIVITY:

| | | SUN | MON | TUE | WED | THU | FRI | SAT |
|---|---|---|---|---|---|---|---|---|
| NOTES: | WK1 | | | | | | | |
| | WK2 | | | | | | | |
| | WK3 | | | | | | | |
| | WK4 | | | | | | | |

ENGAGEMENT ACTIVITY:

| | | SUN | MON | TUE | WED | THU | FRI | SAT |
|---|---|---|---|---|---|---|---|---|
| NOTES: | WK1 | | | | | | | |
| | WK2 | | | | | | | |
| | WK3 | | | | | | | |
| | WK4 | | | | | | | |

ENGAGEMENT ACTIVITY:

| | | SUN | MON | TUE | WED | THU | FRI | SAT |
|---|---|---|---|---|---|---|---|---|
| NOTES: | WK1 | | | | | | | |
| | WK2 | | | | | | | |
| | WK3 | | | | | | | |
| | WK4 | | | | | | | |

# November 2026

23 MONDAY

24 TUESDAY

25 WEDNESDAY

NOTES

26 THURSDAY

Thanksgiving Day

27 FRIDAY

28 SATURDAY

Small Business Saturday

29 SUNDAY

# November 2026

## MONTH IN REVIEW

I AM GRATEFUL FOR

CONNECTED WITH

PERSONAL WINS

WHAT I LEARNED

GOALS MET

PREFERED PLATFORM GROWTH

TOP PERFORMING POST

Doers — gratitude + growth: tell us a win you're thankful for in the Plandipity Doer's Inner Circle (Our Private FB Group).

"DON'T LIMIT YOURSELF. MANY PEOPLE LIMIT THEMSELVES TO WHAT THEY THINK THEY CAN DO. *You can go as far as your mind lets you.* WHAT YOU BELIEVE, REMEMBER, YOU CAN ACHIEVE."

**MARY KAY ASH**

# December 2026

# December 2026

## Business Goal

What's the one thing that will move your business forward this month?

## Personal Goal

What personal win or habit will make life easier or happier?

## Social Media Marketing Planning

### KEY DATES

What holidays, launches, or community events should you post about?

### THIS MONTH'S MARKETING FOCUS

### BUSINESS EVENTS

### PERSONAL EVENTS

PLAN WITH ME!

**Reflect, refresh, and finish strong — scan the QR code for your end-of-year planning video and wrap up the year with purpose.**

# My Tasks This Month

NOTES AND IDEAS

# December 2026

| SUNDAY | MONDAY | TUESDAY | WEDNESDAY |
| --- | --- | --- | --- |
| 29 | 30 | 1 | 2 |
| 6 | 7 | 8 | 9 |
| 13 | 14 | 15 | 16 |
| 20 | 21 | 22 | 23 |
| 27 | 28 | 29 | 30 |

| THURSDAY | FRIDAY | SATURDAY |
| --- | --- | --- |
| 3 | 4 | 5 |
| 10 | 11 | 12 |
| 17 | 18 | 19<br>CONTENT CABOODLE DROPS TODAY! |
| 24 | 25 | 26 |
| 31 | 1 | 2 |

## Notes

## Reminders

**Doer's: be sure to register for weekly We Plan Wednesdays**

# December 2026

## TOP TO-DOS THIS WEEK

- [ ] 
- [ ] 
- [ ] 
- [ ] 
- [ ] 
- [ ] 

## FOLLOW UPS

## APPOINTMENTS

MON

TUE

WED

THU

FRI

SAT

SUN

## SOCIAL MEDIA FOCUS/GOAL THIS WEEK

Reflect,
Reset,
*Refocus!*

## SOCIAL MEDIA ENGAGEMENT PLAN & TRACKER

ENGAGEMENT ACTIVITY:

| | | SUN | MON | TUE | WED | THU | FRI | SAT |
|---|---|---|---|---|---|---|---|---|
| NOTES: | WK1 | | | | | | | |
| | WK2 | | | | | | | |
| | WK3 | | | | | | | |
| | WK4 | | | | | | | |

ENGAGEMENT ACTIVITY:

| | | SUN | MON | TUE | WED | THU | FRI | SAT |
|---|---|---|---|---|---|---|---|---|
| NOTES: | WK1 | | | | | | | |
| | WK2 | | | | | | | |
| | WK3 | | | | | | | |
| | WK4 | | | | | | | |

ENGAGEMENT ACTIVITY:

| | | SUN | MON | TUE | WED | THU | FRI | SAT |
|---|---|---|---|---|---|---|---|---|
| NOTES: | WK1 | | | | | | | |
| | WK2 | | | | | | | |
| | WK3 | | | | | | | |
| | WK4 | | | | | | | |

ENGAGEMENT ACTIVITY:

| | | SUN | MON | TUE | WED | THU | FRI | SAT |
|---|---|---|---|---|---|---|---|---|
| NOTES: | WK1 | | | | | | | |
| | WK2 | | | | | | | |
| | WK3 | | | | | | | |
| | WK4 | | | | | | | |

ENGAGEMENT ACTIVITY:

| | | SUN | MON | TUE | WED | THU | FRI | SAT |
|---|---|---|---|---|---|---|---|---|
| NOTES: | WK1 | | | | | | | |
| | WK2 | | | | | | | |
| | WK3 | | | | | | | |
| | WK4 | | | | | | | |

# December 2026

30 MONDAY

1 TUESDAY

2 WEDNESDAY

NOTES

3 THURSDAY

4 FRIDAY

5 SATURDAY

6 SUNDAY

# December 2026

## TOP TO-DOS THIS WEEK

- 
- 
- 
- 
- 
- 

## FOLLOW UPS

## APPOINTMENTS

MON

TUE

WED

THU

FRI

SAT

SUN

## SOCIAL MEDIA FOCUS/GOAL THIS WEEK

Lessons learned? Yeah, that's a success thing!

# SOCIAL MEDIA ENGAGEMENT PLAN & TRACKER

ENGAGEMENT ACTIVITY:

| | | SUN | MON | TUE | WED | THU | FRI | SAT |
|---|---|---|---|---|---|---|---|---|
| NOTES: | WK1 | | | | | | | |
| | WK2 | | | | | | | |
| | WK3 | | | | | | | |
| | WK4 | | | | | | | |

ENGAGEMENT ACTIVITY:

| | | SUN | MON | TUE | WED | THU | FRI | SAT |
|---|---|---|---|---|---|---|---|---|
| NOTES: | WK1 | | | | | | | |
| | WK2 | | | | | | | |
| | WK3 | | | | | | | |
| | WK4 | | | | | | | |

ENGAGEMENT ACTIVITY:

| | | SUN | MON | TUE | WED | THU | FRI | SAT |
|---|---|---|---|---|---|---|---|---|
| NOTES: | WK1 | | | | | | | |
| | WK2 | | | | | | | |
| | WK3 | | | | | | | |
| | WK4 | | | | | | | |

ENGAGEMENT ACTIVITY:

| | | SUN | MON | TUE | WED | THU | FRI | SAT |
|---|---|---|---|---|---|---|---|---|
| NOTES: | WK1 | | | | | | | |
| | WK2 | | | | | | | |
| | WK3 | | | | | | | |
| | WK4 | | | | | | | |

ENGAGEMENT ACTIVITY:

| | | SUN | MON | TUE | WED | THU | FRI | SAT |
|---|---|---|---|---|---|---|---|---|
| NOTES: | WK1 | | | | | | | |
| | WK2 | | | | | | | |
| | WK3 | | | | | | | |
| | WK4 | | | | | | | |

# December 2026

7 MONDAY Pearl Harbor Remembrance Day

8 TUESDAY

9 WEDNESDAY

NOTES

10 THURSDAY

Hanukkah Begins

11 FRIDAY

12 SATURDAY

13 SUNDAY

# December 2026

## TOP TO-DOS THIS WEEK

- [ ]
- [ ]
- [ ]
- [ ]
- [ ]
- [ ]

## FOLLOW UPS

## APPOINTMENTS

MON

TUE

WED

THU

FRI

SAT

SUN

## SOCIAL MEDIA FOCUS/GOAL THIS WEEK

Refine, don't rewind. That version of you was practice.

## SOCIAL MEDIA ENGAGEMENT PLAN & TRACKER

ENGAGEMENT ACTIVITY:

| | | SUN | MON | TUE | WED | THU | FRI | SAT |
|---|---|---|---|---|---|---|---|---|
| NOTES: | WK1 | | | | | | | |
| | WK2 | | | | | | | |
| | WK3 | | | | | | | |
| | WK4 | | | | | | | |

ENGAGEMENT ACTIVITY:

| | | SUN | MON | TUE | WED | THU | FRI | SAT |
|---|---|---|---|---|---|---|---|---|
| NOTES: | WK1 | | | | | | | |
| | WK2 | | | | | | | |
| | WK3 | | | | | | | |
| | WK4 | | | | | | | |

ENGAGEMENT ACTIVITY:

| | | SUN | MON | TUE | WED | THU | FRI | SAT |
|---|---|---|---|---|---|---|---|---|
| NOTES: | WK1 | | | | | | | |
| | WK2 | | | | | | | |
| | WK3 | | | | | | | |
| | WK4 | | | | | | | |

ENGAGEMENT ACTIVITY:

| | | SUN | MON | TUE | WED | THU | FRI | SAT |
|---|---|---|---|---|---|---|---|---|
| NOTES: | WK1 | | | | | | | |
| | WK2 | | | | | | | |
| | WK3 | | | | | | | |
| | WK4 | | | | | | | |

ENGAGEMENT ACTIVITY:

| | | SUN | MON | TUE | WED | THU | FRI | SAT |
|---|---|---|---|---|---|---|---|---|
| NOTES: | WK1 | | | | | | | |
| | WK2 | | | | | | | |
| | WK3 | | | | | | | |
| | WK4 | | | | | | | |

# December 2026

14 MONDAY

15 TUESDAY

16 WEDNESDAY

NOTES

17 THURSDAY

18 FRIDAY

Hanukkah Ends

19 SATURDAY

20 SUNDAY

# December 2026

## TOP TO-DOS THIS WEEK

- [ ] 
- [ ] 
- [ ] 
- [ ] 
- [ ] 
- [ ] 

## FOLLOW UPS

## APPOINTMENTS

MON

TUE

WED

THU

FRI

SAT

SUN

## SOCIAL MEDIA FOCUS/GOAL THIS WEEK

Celebrate how far you've come.

That *shit* wasn't easy.

You earned that *sparkle!*

# SOCIAL MEDIA ENGAGEMENT PLAN & TRACKER

ENGAGEMENT ACTIVITY:

| | | SUN | MON | TUE | WED | THU | FRI | SAT |
|---|---|---|---|---|---|---|---|---|
| NOTES: | WK1 | | | | | | | |
| | WK2 | | | | | | | |
| | WK3 | | | | | | | |
| | WK4 | | | | | | | |

ENGAGEMENT ACTIVITY:

| | | SUN | MON | TUE | WED | THU | FRI | SAT |
|---|---|---|---|---|---|---|---|---|
| NOTES: | WK1 | | | | | | | |
| | WK2 | | | | | | | |
| | WK3 | | | | | | | |
| | WK4 | | | | | | | |

ENGAGEMENT ACTIVITY:

| | | SUN | MON | TUE | WED | THU | FRI | SAT |
|---|---|---|---|---|---|---|---|---|
| NOTES: | WK1 | | | | | | | |
| | WK2 | | | | | | | |
| | WK3 | | | | | | | |
| | WK4 | | | | | | | |

ENGAGEMENT ACTIVITY:

| | | SUN | MON | TUE | WED | THU | FRI | SAT |
|---|---|---|---|---|---|---|---|---|
| NOTES: | WK1 | | | | | | | |
| | WK2 | | | | | | | |
| | WK3 | | | | | | | |
| | WK4 | | | | | | | |

ENGAGEMENT ACTIVITY:

| | | SUN | MON | TUE | WED | THU | FRI | SAT |
|---|---|---|---|---|---|---|---|---|
| NOTES: | WK1 | | | | | | | |
| | WK2 | | | | | | | |
| | WK3 | | | | | | | |
| | WK4 | | | | | | | |

# December 2026

21 MONDAY

First Day of Winter

22 TUESDAY

23 WEDNESDAY

NOTES

24 THURSDAY

25 FRIDAY

Merry Christmas

26 SATURDAY

National Thank-You Note Day

27 SUNDAY

# December 2026

## TOP TO-DOS THIS WEEK

- [ ] 
- [ ] 
- [ ] 
- [ ] 
- [ ] 
- [ ] 

## FOLLOW UPS

## APPOINTMENTS

MON

TUE

WED

THU

FRI

SAT

SUN

## SOCIAL MEDIA FOCUS/GOAL THIS WEEK

End strong. Begin brighter!

## SOCIAL MEDIA ENGAGEMENT PLAN & TRACKER

ENGAGEMENT ACTIVITY:

| | | SUN | MON | TUE | WED | THU | FRI | SAT |
|---|---|---|---|---|---|---|---|---|
| NOTES: | WK1 | | | | | | | |
| | WK2 | | | | | | | |
| | WK3 | | | | | | | |
| | WK4 | | | | | | | |

ENGAGEMENT ACTIVITY:

| | | SUN | MON | TUE | WED | THU | FRI | SAT |
|---|---|---|---|---|---|---|---|---|
| NOTES: | WK1 | | | | | | | |
| | WK2 | | | | | | | |
| | WK3 | | | | | | | |
| | WK4 | | | | | | | |

ENGAGEMENT ACTIVITY:

| | | SUN | MON | TUE | WED | THU | FRI | SAT |
|---|---|---|---|---|---|---|---|---|
| NOTES: | WK1 | | | | | | | |
| | WK2 | | | | | | | |
| | WK3 | | | | | | | |
| | WK4 | | | | | | | |

ENGAGEMENT ACTIVITY:

| | | SUN | MON | TUE | WED | THU | FRI | SAT |
|---|---|---|---|---|---|---|---|---|
| NOTES: | WK1 | | | | | | | |
| | WK2 | | | | | | | |
| | WK3 | | | | | | | |
| | WK4 | | | | | | | |

ENGAGEMENT ACTIVITY:

| | | SUN | MON | TUE | WED | THU | FRI | SAT |
|---|---|---|---|---|---|---|---|---|
| NOTES: | WK1 | | | | | | | |
| | WK2 | | | | | | | |
| | WK3 | | | | | | | |
| | WK4 | | | | | | | |

# December 2026

28 MONDAY

29 TUESDAY

30 WEDNESDAY

NOTES

31 THURSDAY

1 FRIDAY

New Years Day 2027!

2 SATURDAY

3 SUNDAY

# December 2026

## MONTH IN REVIEW

### I AM GRATEFUL FOR

### CONNECTED WITH

### PERSONAL WINS

### WHAT I LEARNED

### GOALS MET

### PREFERED PLATFORM GROWTH

### TOP PERFORMING POST

Doers — year-end glow-up: share your top December insight in the Plandipity Doer's Inner Circle (Our Private FB Group)

## Notes:

**Notes:**

**Notes:**

**Notes:**

# How To Use This Planner

This planner is your ultimate resource for planning, organizing, and staying consistent with your social media marketing, while still making room for what matters most in your life. The goal is simple: help you grow your business and live the lifestyle that fits you best.

You'll find social media prompts, content resources, weekly layouts, and planning tools designed to keep you aligned with your goals. Think of it as your all-in-one guide to elevating your life and business in 2026.

**Here's how to make the most of it:**

**My Goals & Action Steps**
Start the year by writing down your big business and personal goals. Then map out the action steps and habits that will actually move you toward them.

**Monthly Dividers & QR Codes**
Each month begins with a motivational divider and a QR code linking to a special planning video. Use it to plan your social media content with me and get your monthly pep talk and resources.

**Monthly Planning & To-Do List**
Use this page to outline your top priorities, anchor your focus, and set your goals for the month.

**Monthly Calendars**
A two-page spread for mapping your days, noting holidays, tracking Plandipity Doers reminders (like Content Caboodle drops and We Plan Wednesday calls), and giving yourself a big-picture view.

**Weekly Planning Pages & Engagement Tracker**
Each week opens with space to sort your top tasks, follow-ups, appointments, and social media goals. You'll also find a clear section for engagement intentions, clients to connect with, prospects to follow up with, and groups or accounts to show up in.

**Weekly Layouts**
A two-page spread for daily scheduling and prioritization, not just for marketing but for your life. When you love what you're building, staying organized becomes a form of self-support.

**End-of-Month Reflection**
Capture your biggest wins, discoveries, lessons, and growth areas so you roll into each new month with clarity and confidence.

This is more than a planner—it's your glitter-dusted roadmap to staying consistent, creative, and aligned all year long.